A Dream of Stone
Marguerite Yourcenar

Introduction by John Knight

Contents

A Dream of Stone

David Zwirner Books

ekphrasis

Introduction

John Knight

Born in Brussels in 1903, Marguerite Yourcenar never attended school. Ten days after she was born, her mother died of puerperal fever and she was raised by her patrician father, Michel, and her grandmother. Michel realized early that Yourcenar possessed a precocious mind and furnished her with Latin and Greek, read with her the French classics, hired competent tutors, and instilled in her a passion for travel. The relationship was deeply formative, though Yourcenar later characterized him as a man "perpetually absent without leave." When Yourcenar announced as a teenager that she intended to be a writer, Michel delivered her manuscripts to editors and published her early collections of poetry at his own expense, despite his increasing penury. Together they spent an evening rearranging the letters of her given name, Marguerite de Crayencour, until they landed on a near-perfect anagram, "for the pleasure of the Y," she would say.

Critical acclaim arrived with the publication of her first two novellas, *Alexis* in 1929, and *Coup de Grâce* in 1939, and when *Memoirs of Hadrian* appeared in 1951, Yourcenar became truly renowned. Her literary output was prolific: novels and short stories, plays and a three-volume memoir, essays on Pindar, Selma Lagerlöf, and C. P. Cavafy, translations of Virginia Woolf, James Baldwin, and Yukio Mishima. Though she was fluent and eloquent in English, she always wrote in French. She prized expression of emotion over abstraction and intellectualization, citing the early influence of Apollinaire, Cocteau, and especially Valéry. She thought Thomas Mann's

The Holy Sinner was a masterpiece, and reread Hardy's *Far from the Madding Crowd* annually. She disliked Colette ("a Parisian concierge" in matters of eroticism) and Sade ("his lack of realism vexes me"). Of magical realism: "They are like factory products." She preferred the feminine form of "afternoon" (*la après-midi*). She was a good cook who likened making bread to writing and despised supermarkets, "with their enamel-painted walls … and the mechanical music that flows like poor-quality syrup." She rode horses and was a legendary hypochondriac. When she was inducted into the Académie Française in 1981—the first woman to ever join those prestigious ranks—she declined the typical uniform and wore a black velvet skirt and cape designed by Yves Saint Laurent, and refused the customary gift of a sword.

Yourcenar once remarked that all her stories and characters were in her by the time she was twenty, but not actually written for another thirty or forty years (her two great novels—*Memoirs of Hadrian* and *The Abyss*—were published when she was forty-eight and sixty-five, respectively). "I had hardly any knowledge of history and none of life to do anything with them," she recalled. While Yourcenar's major works are sustained, encompassing ventures into the past and the human heart, the pieces collected here read almost as curiosities, animating her approach to the arts. They reveal not only the themes that preoccupied Yourcenar as a novelist and thinker (time, desire, dreams, originality, authenticity), but also her method as an artist herself.

When Yourcenar was thirty-three years old and living in Paris, she met Grace Frick, an American who offered her refuge when the war broke out in 1939. The two bought a house together on Mount Desert Island in Maine in 1950, and it was there, between long episodes of travel, that Yourcenar wrote most of her books. The house was small—a cottage really—that the two dubbed Petite Plaisance, "a country house such as I could have had anywhere in the world." On the walls she hung an unremarkable Chinese engraving given to her by a friend, two paintings by Marie Laurencin, a portrait of herself by Han Harloff, and several etchings by Piranesi.

Shortly after she moved into this house and finished *Memoirs of Hadrian*, Yourcenar began her essay on that incomparable engraver. The piece serves as more than just a primer. "All the eighteenth-century angles of incidence and reflection intersect in the strange linear universe of Giovanni Battista Piranesi," she writes. Yourcenar proves this thesis by considering the whole of Piranesi's works, only then turning to the alluringly fantastical *Prisons*. The pleasure of reading Yourcenar is watching her levy her formidable learning on a subject like this. She considers the effects of the Baroque on Piranesi's pre-Baroque intuitions, his Goethean desire to preserve Roman antiquity with "'the greatest possible exactitude,'" his architectural poetry of decay, and that "grotesque contrast between papal pomp and antique grandeur on the one hand, and on the other the miseries and absurdities of contemporary Roman life."

Finally, she comes to Time: "Piranesi's image of the ruin does not release a discourse on the grandeur and decadence of empires and the instability of human affairs," she writes, "but rather a meditation on the duration or the slow erosion of things, on the opaque identity of the block continuing, within the monument, its long existence of stone *as stone*."

This ineffable and fragile aspect of continuity is one of Yourcenar's great themes, one she takes up with relish. In "Sistine" she constructs four different perspectives: three from young male lovers and models of Michelangelo, and one from the maestro himself about a fourth beloved. When Michelangelo completed the Sistine Chapel, there was considerable controversy around the twenty *Ignudi* scattered throughout the frescoes. Yourcenar imagines her way into what these young men must have meant to Michelangelo for him to drape them along the corners of that vaulted ceiling with nary a toga in sight, and the inherent cruelty of desire when mixed with ambition. Years later in Maine, Yourcenar remarked on some "unpublished" nudes of Michelangelo's hanging on the wall of Petite Plaisance, "which for me represent the whirlwind of natural forces in human terms."

The piece, written when Yourcenar was twenty-eight, is one of the first instances of her casting aside her own time and body, and inhabiting those entirely foreign. "No one possesses anyone," Yourcenar prompts Michelangelo to assert, "(even sinners cannot achieve that), and since art is the only true possession, it is less a matter of possessing than of re-creating a person.... Gherardo, you are now more beautiful than yourself." Despite her somewhat grand proclamations on love and death, Yourcenar here hones a remarkable talent to live inside the people of the past and to re-create deceased feelings and relationships.

Once this voice is inside your head, it is difficult to look up at those naked shoulders and thighs and not feel something of the maestro's great passion for what he was painting—for his model and for the art itself. Such is Yourcenar's effect: an invitation into the sensation of a work's genesis, and especially an encounter with the desire at once satiated and refused by art. And there is something else here, too, a theme that winds its way through Yourcenar's writing, about the interplay between a work and time itself. "At every instant," Michelangelo asserts, "the marble in which we think we have preserved a form of perishable life returns to its place in nature, through erosion, patina, and the play of light and shadow over planes which thought they were abstract but are in fact only the surface of a stone." With this swerve, Yourcenar uses the idealized notion about the timelessness of art as a foil, and sneaks in a more subtle concept about time as an agent of art.

Nearly twenty-five years later, she takes up this idea more fully in "That Mighty Sculptor, Time." Here Time is the shaping force, and the sculptor's hand only a brief interlude in the true fate of a stone. She calls this an "involuntary beauty," imparted by the elements or neglect or sabotage, and maintains that no matter the decay, the sculptor's intention "affirms itself forever in the ruin of things." In the final paragraph she goes one step further by evoking the marble statues lost to the sea in the shipwrecks of antiquity. The gestures bestowed on these statues "proved to be only a brief episode between their incalculable duration as rock in the bosom of the mountain and their long existence as stone lying at the bottom of the sea." Even those most enduring monuments are only momentarily arrested instances of form.

Marguerite Yourcenar's most revered book is a fictional memoir of the great Roman emperor Hadrian. Written as a letter from the dying emperor to Marcus Aurelius, his heir and adopted son, the book imagines Hadrian's life in lush detail, measuring the historical against private longing, ambition, and sorrow. Early on Yourcenar causes Hadrian to reflect on sleep, and especially on dreams. "What interests me here," Hadrian muses, "is the specific mystery of sleep partaken of for itself alone, the inevitable plunge risked each night by the naked man, solitary and unarmed, into an ocean where everything changes, the colors, the densities, and even the rhythm of breathing, and where we meet the dead." This might as well serve as a description of Yourcenar's own work. Her writing is invariably a journey to a different time and place. Her stories and essays are set in Rembrandt's Amsterdam, Michelangelo's Rome, or Huguenot France, and always attempt to imagine the interior life of someone scraping their own humanity against the real demands of their time.

To the end of her life, Yourcenar refused the label "historical novel," insisting that the past was merely a vehicle by which a particular quality of human emotion could be accessed. "The decisive moment for a writer," she said in a late interview, "occurs when geology supersedes history. I mean that this happens when one digs ever more profoundly into the distant epochs of history." "Tone and Language in the Historical Novel" is a remarkable exposition of this process. Here Yourcenar outlines the linguistic method she developed to write novels set in the past that would be genuine to the time they portray. Masquerading as a simple explanation of how she approached her own fictions, the piece offers a sly critique of the medium an artist chooses, and how method and material authenticity are a prerequisite for artistic resonance.

"It has not been sufficiently emphasized," Yourcenar writes in the opening paragraph, "that although we possess an enormous mass of written documents, and also visual documents, from the past, nothing is left to us of *voices* before the first nasal-sounding phonograph records of the nineteenth century." The rigor that Yourcenar then exhibits in parsing her own writing only reinforces the notion that what is thoroughly delightful in, say, *Memoirs of Hadrian* is something earned by a geologist, rather than a historian. This is the same sensitivity to the sight and sound that she organizes in her essay on Piranesi, how the "formidable silence" of the *Prisons* leaves the viewer vulnerable to the lightest footstep, just as among all the twisting stairs and passageways, there is nowhere to hide, no escape from sight.

This kind of practiced *embodiment* is precisely what makes Yourcenar's novels—many of them from the perspective of men who live in a different time, practice a specialized profession, and love other men—so alive. It is as though she could dream her way into other minds, not to accurately re-create them, but to imbue them with color, densities, and the rhythm of breathing. For instance, of all the aspects of Albrecht Dürer that one might take up in an essay on his work—that he trained as a goldsmith, drew his rhinoceros without ever seeing a real one, obsessively created self-portraits—Yourcenar chooses, or perhaps cannot overlook, a small watercolor painting and brief description of one of his dreams. It is the only account she knows from the sixteenth century in which such a thing is presented without polishing: "the extraordinary account of a dream which is nothing but a dream." Just as the vocabulary that was available to Hadrian or Zeno in their respective times provides a contemporary novelist particular access to their emotions, so does this sketch of water columns and its attendant description give us a genuine glimpse of a human being *alive* in a particular time and place.

This is the same intuitive reading that provides Yourcenar her insight on Piranesi. "What we are shown here," she writes frankly about his *Prisons*, "is a dream."

And not just any dream, but "a dream of stone." The incoherence, intoxication, negations, and levitations in these images are all framed within a kind of oneiric logic of blocks, pavers, and tiles interlocking and tessellating up and up and up. Piranesi's calculations are exact, yet his proportions false; everyday construction devices are recast in the guise of torture instruments; and the true horror of these etchings, unnoticed at first, resides in the indifference of the tiny groups of people "strolling along the cantilevers or climbing the stairs," ignorant that they are teetering on the "brink of the abyss." This is the beguiling achievement of Piranesi, and Yourcenar extends it to the larger endeavor of making art: by manipulating space and time, the artist affects the same mysterious authenticity often associated—unnervingly, revealingly—with our dreams.

"What also reassures us," Hadrian says, "is that sleep heals us of fatigue, but heals us by the most radical of means in arranging that we cease temporarily to exist. There, as elsewhere, the pleasure and the art consist in conscious surrender to that blissful unconsciousness, and in accepting to be slightly less strong, less light, less heavy and less definite than our waking selves." In each of these pieces, Yourcenar offers a similar invitation, one at once radical and brief, to engage some other consciousness, some other dream.

The Dark Brain of Piranesi

"The dark brain of Piranesi . . ." said Victor Hugo in one of his poems. The man to whom this brain belonged was born in 1720 into one of those Venetian families in which the crafts, the professions, and the Church harmoniously cohabited. His stonecutter father; his uncle Matteo Lucchesi, an engineer and architect from whom young Giovanni Battista acquired the rudiments of technical knowledge which sustained his later work; his brother Angelo, a Carthusian who taught him Roman history— all helped shape various aspects of his future as an artist. Uncle Matteo in particular was, one might say, a sort of early and rather mediocre version of Piranesi himself: from him the nephew inherited not only an erroneous theory as to the Etruscan origins of Greek architecture, which he stubbornly defended all his life, but also his respect for the art of architecture considered as a form of divine creation. To the end of his days, the great engraver, who was the interpreter and virtually the inventor of Rome's tragic beauty, proudly and perhaps somewhat arbitrarily assumed the title of Venetian architect: *architectus venetianus*. It was also in Venice that he practiced painting in the studios of the Valeriani brothers, and even more significantly of the Bibbienas, those poets and virtuosi of theater architecture. Finally, having returned to Venice for several months in 1744, at a time when he was already beginning to establish himself in Rome, he seems to have frequented Tiepolo's atelier; in any case, he certainly came under the influence of this last master of the Venetian grand manner.

It was in 1740, at the age of twenty, that Piranesi, as a draftsman attached to the household of the Venetian ambassador Foscarini, first passed through the Porta del Popolo. No man, if we would than have foretold his future, better deserved a triumphal entrance into the Eternal City. As a matter of fact, the young artist began by studying engraving with a certain Giuseppe Vasi, a conscientious manufacturer of views of Rome, who found his pupil far too good a painter to be a good engraver. With reason, since engraving, in the hands of Vasi and of so many other manufacturers of prints, was hardly more than a rapid and economic process of mechanical reproduction for which excessive talent was more dangerous than useful. Nonetheless, and for reasons partly external, such as the difficulty of mak-ing a career as an architect and designer in the rather somnolent Rome of the eighteenth century, partly due to the artist's temperament itself, engraving becomes Piranesi's sole means of expression: the velleities of the painter of stage sets, the impassioned vocation of the architect apparently gave way; in reality, they im-posed on his burin a certain style and certain themes. At the same time, the artist has found his subject, which is Rome, and with which for nearly thirty-eight years he will fill the thousand or so plates of his descriptive *oeuvre*. In the more limited group of early works, gov-erned, on the contrary, by a free architectural fantasy, and in particular in the inspired *Imaginary Prisons*, he will audaciously combine elements which are Roman;

he will transpose the substance of Rome into the realm of the irrational.

Apart from the brief absence of 1744, when he returned to Venice for the reason which invariably compels artists and poets to return home, lack of money, Piranesi never left Rome again except to explore its immediate environs and for two peregrinations that were more considerable, especially in those days of bad roads—one to Umbria in 1764, to investigate the Etruscan antiquities of Corneto and Chiusi; the other in 1774, to the Kingdom of Naples, where Pompeii and Herculaneum, recently discovered, and Paestum, rediscovered even more recently, were then brand-new attractions. Piranesi has left several haunting sketches of the dead streets of Pompeii; he brought back some splendid drawings from Paestum, which prove once again that the artist's eye and hand are wiser than his "mind," for he continued to the last to regard Greek architecture as a simple succedaneum of Etruscan, highly inferior to the art of the Roman mason. This theory, less indefensible at the time than today because of the learned world's almost complete ignorance of Greece itself, involved him in a long dispute with certain antiquarians of the day, among others the fervent Winckelmann, a lover and theoretician of Greek statuary. The incomparable abbé assigned Greece first place, as is fitting, but in an almost complete absence of Hellenic originals of the best periods, he happened to exalt certain mediocre Hellenistic or Greco-Roman copies as characteristic of Greek art, and to fall into systematization and error in his turn. This futile dispute doubtless served Piranesi as a stimulant or else as a kind of safety valve; it deserves to be forgotten, if it were not interesting to see it as the confrontation over an ill-framed issue of the two men who revivified our conception of the antique.

We know some of Piranesi's successive Roman domiciles: first of all the Palazzo di Venezia, the Serenissima's embassy to the Holy See at the time; then the shop on the Corso where, having returned from his visit to his native city and quarreled with his family, who had cut off his funds, he set himself up as the agent of the Venetian print dealer Giuseppe Wagner; finally, the studio in the via Felice (today the via Sistina), where the second states of the *Prisons* were on sale at their creator's for the price of 20 écus, and where Piranesi breathed his last, a thriving artist covered with honors, a member of the Academy of St. Luke since 1757, ennobled by Clement XIII in 1767. Like so many men of taste then settled in Rome, the Cavaliere Piranesi did not disdain to practice the profitable trade of dealing in antiquities; certain engravings of his *Vasi, Candelabri, Cippi, Sarcofagi, Tripodi, Lucerne ed Ornamenti antichi* served to circulate the image of one or another splendid item among enlightened amateurs. He appears to have been chiefly surrounded by a group of foreign artists and connoisseurs: the good-natured Hubert Robert, who sometimes seems to have undertaken to retranslate Piranesi's Baroque Rome into rococo terms, the publisher Bouchard, who printed the

first states of the *Prisons* and the *Antiquities of Rome*—
"Buzzard," as Piranesi spelled it, and no doubt lisped it
as well, in the Venetian fashion. Of the English colony,
Piranesi's circle included the architect and decorator
Robert Adam, who adapted Italian classicism to British tastes and habits, and that other London architect
George Dance, who was inspired, it is said, by the *Imaginary Prisons* to design the very real dungeons of Newgate.
The thread which continued to attach Piranesi to Venice
during these years was the friendship of the papal and
banking family, the Rezzonicos: Pope Clement XIII employed him as a decorator and appointed him architect
for certain projects at St. John Lateran, which, however,
were never carried out or even begun. In 1764, one of the
Pope's nephews, Cardinal Rezzonico, entrusted Piranesi
with the task of partly rebuilding and entirely redecorat-
ing the Church of Santa Maria Aventina, the property of
the Order of the Knights of Malta, of which he was the
Grand Prior. This modest commission required less majesty than grace: Piranesi transformed the little façade of
the church and the great walls of the Piazza dei Cavalieri
di Malta into a harmonious ensemble embellished with
escutcheons and trophies in which, as in his *Grotesques*,
certain ancient architectural elements combined with
a Venetian whimsicality. This was the sole occasion this
dedicated architect would have to express himself in actual marble and stone.

What we know of Piranesi's private life is limited
to his marriage to a gardener's daughter, a handsome

young woman with fine black eyes whom the artist regarded as incarnating the pure Roman type. Legend has it that he met this Angelica Pasquini in the then nobly deserted ruins of the Forum, where he was sketching on that particular evening, and took her for his wife after having possessed her then and there on ground sacred to the memory of Antiquity. If the anecdote is authentic, this violent dreamer must have imagined he was enjoying the favors of Magna Tellus herself, Dea Roma incarnate in the solid flesh of this young *popolana*. A different but not necessarily contradictory version informs us that the artist urged marriage when he learned that the beauty would bring a dowry of 150 piastres. Whatever the case, this Angelica gave him three children, who continued his own labors without genius but assiduously: Francesco, the most gifted, followed his father in uniting the engraver's profession with that of archaeologist and dealer in antiquities; it was he who obtained for Gustave III of Sweden the mediocre (and in some cases dubious) marbles which today form a touching little eighteenth-century collection "of an enlightened amateur" in a room of the Royal Palace in Stockholm.

It is a Frenchman, one Jacques-Guillaume Legrand, whom we may thank for gathering from Francesco Piranesi's lips most of our details as to his father's life, views, and character; what remains of the artist's writings confirms his observations. We see a man of passionate feelings, intoxicated by work, careless of his health and his comfort, disdaining the *malaria* of the Roman

Campagna, sustaining himself on nothing but cold rice during his long sojourns in such solitary and unhealthy sites as, at the time, Hadrian's Villa or the ruins of Albano and Cora, and lighting his scanty campfire only once a week in order to waste none of the time reserved for his explorations and his works. "The verisimilitude and the vigor of his effects," notes Jacques-Guillaume Legrand, with that sober pertinence which is the mark of eighteenth-century intellectuals, "the accurate projection of his shadows and their transparency, or the fortunate liberties taken in this regard, the very indication of shadings of color are due to the exact observation which he was to make from nature, either under the burning sun or by moonlight." It is easy to imagine, beneath the unendurable noonday sun or at an almost luminous midnight, this observer on the prowl for the ineffable, seeking in this apparent immobility whatever moves and changes, scrutinizing ruins to discover the secret of a highlight, the place for a crosshatching, as others were to do in order to dig up treasures or to raise ghosts. This great overworked artisan died in Rome in 1778, of a neglected kidney ailment; he was buried at the expense of Cardinal Rezzonico in the Church of Santa Maria Aventina, where his tomb may be visited today. A portrait inserted as a frontispiece to the *Prisons* shows him in around his thirtieth year, hair close-cropped, eyes intense, features somewhat soft, very Italian, and very much a man of the eighteenth century, despite the naked shoulders and pectorals of a Roman bust. From the

viewpoint of chronology alone, we may note that he was
a contemporary of Rousseau, of Diderot, and of Casanova, and the elder by a generation of the Goya of the
Caprichos, of the Goethe of the *Roman Elegies*, of Sade the
obsessed, and of that great prison reformer Beccaria. All
the eighteenth-century angles of incidence and reflection intersect in the strange linear universe of Giovanni
Battista Piranesi.

At first glance it seems possible to make a selection from
Piranesi's almost overabundant production—to relegate,
for instance, as certain timorous critics of the past have
done, the sixteen plates of the *Prisons* to the wing reserved for madness and delirium, and to extol, on the
contrary, in the *Views* and the *Antiquities of Rome*,[1] a logical discourse, a reality scrupulously observed and nobly
transcribed. Or else, fashion having as always intervened
and paradoxically reversed the terms, to regard the *Prisons* as the sole series in which the great engraver freely
expressed and exercised his genius, and to degrade the
Antiquities and *Views* to the level of admirably fluent com-
monplaces fabricated to please a clientele in love with
historical clichés and famous sites, and thereby certain

1   It is for the sake of convenience and simplification that we here designate as *Views of Rome* or *Antiquities of Rome* the countless representations
of ancient monuments Piranesi has left us. Aside from the *Antichità
Romane* and the *Vedute* and the *Varie Vedute di Roma*, a complete list of
Piranesi's descriptive work would also include the *Antichità Romane de'
Tempi della Repubblica*, the *Antichità d'Albano*, the *Antichità di Cora*, the
engravings which embellish his great polemical study *Della Magnificenza
ed Architettura de' Romani*, and several other series as well.

of a ready market. And of course it can never be said too often that the voluminous series of *Views* and *Antiquities* represented, for the eighteenth-century dealer and connoisseur, the equivalent of the coffee-table albums of artistic photographs offered nowadays to the tourist eager to confirm or complement his memories, or to the sedentary reader who dreams of faraway places. We might almost say that in relation to the engravers who preceded him, the Piranesi of the *Views* occupies the position enjoyed, among his mediocre and literal confrères, by the virtuoso photographer who exploits backlighting, effects of mist or twilight, unexpected and revealing angles ... And yet we should be completely denaturing Piranesi's productions by establishing for them a scale of values ranging from the quasi-artisanal level of his album *On Various Fashions of Embellishing Chimneypieces*, or from his diagrams of clocks or gondolas, to the still semicommercial stage of the *Views* and *Antiquities of Rome*, and finally attaining, in the *Prisons*, a kind of pure subjective vision. In reality, the slender album of the *Prisons*, with its dark images resulting, it is said, from a bout of fever, also corresponds to an established genre and almost to a vogue: a painter like Pannini, engravers like the Bibbienas, compiled at the time or even earlier their audacious decors for operas or imaginary tragedies, constructions consisting of real architectural elements skillfully juxtaposed with dream-like perspectives. Furthermore, Piranesi's artisan drawings attest not only to the same temperament but to the same obsessions as his boldest or most powerful masterpieces. The chimneypiece covered with symbols and fabulous animals in the *Arte d'adornare i cammini*, worthy of imprisoning fire in the cabinet of a Rosicrucian, is indeed from the same hand which drew the gigantic lions of Plate v of the *Prisons*; the study of a project for a carriage attests to the same exquisite sensibility as the complicated schema of the *Grand Thermae of Hadrian's Villa*. Without the help of his more artisanal work, we should perhaps fail to place his major productions in their period and in the fashion of the time; we should overlook in him the part of the clever decorator. Without the *Antiquities* and *Views*, the phantasmagorical universe of the *Prisons* would seem too studied, too factitious; we should not discern in it the authentic materials reappearing obsessionally amid his own nightmares. Without the almost demonic boldness of the *Prisons*, we should hesitate to recognize, in the apparent classicism of the *Views* and the *Antiquities*, the *deep song* of a meditation on the life and death of forms at once visual and metaphysical.

The subjects of Piranesi's descriptive engravings fall into two categories, which of course intersect. On one hand, the Baroque edifice, still new or virtually so: the rectilinear façade with its unbroken walls; the obelisk dividing perspectives; the street where rows of palaces produce a slightly curving line, which is one of the miracles of Rome; the ellipse or the irregular polygon of the bare, flat piazzas; the parallelepiped of the interior views of basilicas; the cylinder and the sliced-off sphere of

cupola-churches' interiors; the rotunda revolving open
to the sky; the monumental fountain whose rounded ba-
sin imitates the curve of a wave; the smooth and polished
facings of floors and walls. On the other hand, the ruins
already fifteen centuries old: broken stone and crumbling brick; the collapsing vault that welcomes light's
intrusion; the tunnel of dark rooms opening in the distance on daylight streaming through a broken wall; the
overhanging plinth, suspended on the brink of its col-
lapse, the great broken rhythm of aqueducts and colon-
nades; temples and basilicas lying open and as though
turned inside out by the depredations of time and of
man, so that the interior has now become a kind of exterior, everywhere invaded by space like a ship by water.
Piranesi establishes an equilibrium of communicating
vessels between what is for him still modern and what is
already, for him as for us, the antique, between the new
monument solidly established in a time which is still his
own, and the monument already touching the last extremity of its trajectory through the centuries. If it tumbled down, this *St.-Paul's-outside-the-Walls* would be no
different from the ancient temple to which its columns
once belonged; in ruins, this *Colonnade of St. Peter's*
would closely resemble the porticoes of Nero's Cir-
cus, which it has replaced. Intact, this *Temple of Venus*
or these *Baths of Caracalla*, by the luxury of their marbles, by the abundance of stuccos and the prolifera-
tion of gigantic statues, would correspond to the same
preoccupations with pomp and prestige as an edifice

by Bernini. The genius of the Baroque has given Piranesi the intuition of that pre-Baroque architecture created by Imperial Rome; it has preserved him from the cold academicism of his successors, with whom he is sometimes confused, and for whom the monuments of Antiquity are no more than scholarly texts. It is to the Baroque that Piranesi, in his *Views*, owes these sudden breakdowns of equilibrium, this very deliberate readjustment of perspective, this analysis of mass which is for its period a conquest as considerable as the Impressionists' analysis of light later on. To the Baroque as well he owes these great unexpected interplays of shadow and shafts of light, these shifting illuminations, so different from the skies of eternity which the Renaissance painters set behind their imitation-antique palaces and temples, and which a nineteenth-century Corot was to rediscover in his Italian period. Finally, it is to the Baroque that Piranesi owes a sense of the superhuman which he carries to dizzy heights in the *Prisons*.

Of course, the creator of the *Views* and the *Antiquities of Rome* invented neither the craze for ruins nor the love of Rome. A century before him, Poussin and Claude Gellée had also discovered Rome with a foreigner's fresh eyes; their work was nourished on these inexhaustible sites. But while for a Claude, for a Poussin, Rome had been chiefly an admirable background for personal reverie or else for discourse of a general order—in short, a sacred site purified of any contemporary contingency, situated halfway to the divine country of Fable, it is the

City itself, the City in all its aspects and in all its implications, from the most banal to the most unwonted, that Piranesi has fixed at a certain moment of the eighteenth century, in a thousand plates at once anecdotal and visionary. He has not merely explored the ancient monuments as a draftsman looking for a point of view; he has explored the remains in person, in part to unearth the antiquities he makes a business of, but above all to penetrate the secret of their foundations, to learn and to demonstrate how they were built. He is an archaeologist in a period when the word itself is not in common usage. To the last, he docilely follows custom, which consists in numbering on the plates each part of the structure, each fragment of ornament still in place, and making certain explanatory notes in the lower margin correspond to them, without its ever occurring to him, as it certainly would to an artist nowadays, that these schoolbook specifications or engineering diagrams might diminish the aesthetic or picturesque value of his work. "When I realized that in Rome the majority of the ancient monuments were lying forsaken in fields or gardens, or even now serving as a quarry for new structures, I resolved to preserve their memory with the help of my engravings. I have therefore attempted to exercise the greatest possible exactitude." There is already something Goethean about this sentence in its assertion of a modest desire to be useful. To grasp the importance of this rescue work, we must recall that at least a third of the monuments drawn by Piranesi have since vanished, and that what remains has most often been despoiled of the surfacings and stuccos then still in place, or again modified, and restored, sometimes clumsily, between the end of the eighteenth century and our own time. Nowadays when artists believe they are liberating themselves by breaking the links which connect them to the outside world, it is worth noting what a precise solicitude for the object contemplated is at the source of Piranesi's almost hallucinatory masterpieces.

Many painters of genius have been architects as well; very few have thought solely in terms of architecture in their painted, drawn, or engraved work. Further, certain painters who have also tried to be archaeologists—the Ingres of *Stronice*, for example—have generally produced no more than a cheap and disappointing imitation. On the contrary, Piranesi's studies as an architect taught him to reflect thoroughly and continuously in terms of balance and weight, of blocks and of mortar. His antiquarian research, furthermore, accustomed him to recognize in each fragment of antiquity the singularities or specifications of kind; they were for him what the dissection of cadavers is for a painter of the nude. It seems in particular that the passion for building, repressed in this man limited throughout his career to the two dimensions of a sheet of copper, rendered him particularly apt at rediscovering in a ruined monument the energy which originally raised it from the ground. We might almost say that the raw materials, in the *Antiquities*, are expressed for their own sake: Piranesi's image

of the ruin does not release a discourse on the grandeur
and decadence of empires and the instability of human
affairs, but rather a meditation on the duration or the
slow erosion of things, on the opaque identity of the
block continuing, within the monument, its long existence of stone *as stone*. Conversely, for Piranesi Rome's
majesty survives in a broken vault, rather than in an as-
sociation of ideas with some buried Caesar. The edifice
is sufficient unto itself; it is at once the drama and the
drama's decor, the site of a dialogue between the human
will still inscribed in these enormous masonries, inert
mineral energy, and irrevocable Time.

This secret metaphysical poetry sometimes seems, in
the hands of this compatriot of Arcimboldo, to end by
producing double images, due not so much to caprice as
to the intensity of his visionary gaze. The collapsed cu-
pola of *Canopus* and that of the *Temple of Diana at Baiae*
are the fractured skull, the bony casement from which
dangle filaments of grass and weeds; the *Antonine Column* and *Trajan's Column* irresistibly suggest, in this
oeuvre so apparently lacking in eroticism, certain frenzied verses by Théophile Gautier on the Vendôme Column; the obelisk lying in sections at the foot of the *Palazzo Barberini* is a corpse hacked to pieces by nameless
bravi. Even more often, instead of simply identifying the
man-made shape with the human body, visual metaphor
tends to reinstate the edifice within the ensemble of natural forces, of which our most complicated architectures

are never anything but a partial and unconscious micro-
cosm. The ruin leans against the new palace like a dead
log against living trees; the half-collapsed dome seems
to be a mound scaled by a troop of bushes; buildings assume the aspect of lava, of sponge, having reached that
degree of undifferentiated matter where we no longer
know if this pebble picked up on the beach has once
been carved by the hand of man or was fashioned thus
by the tides. The extraordinary *Fountain Wall of Hadrian's
Tomb* is a cliff against which the centuries have washed
and broken; the empty *Coliseum* is an extinct crater. This
sense of great natural metamorphoses is perhaps never
more evident in Piranesi than in the drawings which he
brought back from Paestum, and which his son Francesco honorably completed after his death, peopling
them with shepherds and Theocritan cattle. But here
violence gives way to peace; metaphor is dissolved into
a simple affirmation of the object contemplated. Greece,
which the draftsman approached without knowing it,
suffuses these images with a robust beauty at once in-
dividual and abstract, so different from Rome's simultaneously utilitarian and romantic grandeur. The ruined
temple is not merely a wreck on the sea of forms; it itself
is nature: its shafts are the equivalent of a sacred wood;
its rhythms of projection and recession are a melody in
the Dorian mode; its wreckage remains a precept, an
admonition, an order of things. The work of this tragic
poet of architecture comes to its close upon this ecstasy
of serenity.

Before leaving the *Views*, let us consider for a moment, magnifying glass in hand, the minuscule humanity which gesticulates on the ruins or in the streets of Rome. *Fantoccini, burattini, puppi*: these ladies in paniered gowns, these gentlemen wearing swords and capes *à la française*, these hooded monks and these *monsignori* belonging to the repertoire of eighteenth-century Italy—they give off an atmosphere of Goldoni or of Casanova, a fragrance more Venetian than Roman. With these characters from genre painting reduced to infinitesimal proportions by the enormity of the edifices, Piranesi has mingled the picaresque personnel of the Roman Campagna, muleteers, Trastevere girls lugging their broods, beggars, cripples, and almost everywhere the hairy and agile goatherds, scarcely more human than their flocks. Nowhere has the artist attempted, as have so many Baroque or Romantic painters of Rome before or since, to harmonize human nobility and gravity with architectural dignity. It is a rare thing if, here and there, a small figure of a handsome youth standing or prone, solitary wanderer, dreamer, or simply local guide, suggests among these human will-o'-the-wisps the equivalent of an ancient statue. "Instead of studying from the nude or from the only good models, which are those of Greek statuary," writes Piranesi's first biographer, Bianconi, toward the end of the eighteenth century, "he preferred to draw the most wretched cripples and the most hideous hunchbacks to be found in Rome. When he had occasion to find one of these monsters begging upon some church doorstep, he rejoiced as if he had discovered a new Apollo Belvedere." The presence of these vagabonds sometimes endows Piranesi's deserted sites with a suggestion of danger. In one of the plates of the *Antiquities*, two dancer-like graverobbers are quarreling over a skeleton almost as graceful as themselves; another thief has snatched up the skull, while two steps away, under the split lid of the sarcophagus, a carved bucranium adds an image of the animal death's-head to the human one. The ruin literally seethes: each new glance reveals a new group of human insects rummaging through the rubble or the brush. Rags, cowls, and flounces consort in the shining church interiors, not to mention the dogs snapping at each other and scratching their fleas at the very foot of the holy altars. Piranesi's strollers and prowlers betray that easy, devil-may-care, occasionally alarming behavior, Mephistophelean before Goethe invented his Mephistopheles, which, if we are to believe painters from Watteau to Magnasco and from Hogarth to Goya, was typical of the century from beginning to end.

The grotesque contrast between papal pomp and antique grandeur on the one hand, and on the other the miseries and absurdities of contemporary Roman life, had already been felt some two hundred years earlier by the Du Bellay of *Les Regrets*, who was also one of the first poets to celebrate *in situ* the majesty of Rome's ruins. It erupts again in the strident opening of Voltaire's *Voyages de Scarmentado* ("I left Rome, highly pleased with the architecture of St. Peter's"); we will encounter it all over again a century later in Belli. It would seem only natural to attribute to the creator of the *Views* the same intention of mocking counterpoint, but these little characters from the comedy of manners or picaresque romance are too stereotyped in aspect and format for us to assume in Piranesi any depth of irony or well-concealed disdain: this trivial *hoi polloi* and this preening world of fashion simply served him, as so many engravers of his period, to accentuate the elevation of the vaults and the depth of the perspectives. At most they constituted for him a *scherzo* contrasting with the architecture's solemn *largo*. And yet these homunculi whom we discover absurdly perched on the dizzying stories of the *Prisons* correspond too closely to a certain sense of mockery and of the futility of human life not to acquire, at least implicitly, a value as very minor symbols; not to remind us of a half-mathematical, half-satirical badinage which obsessed certain of the best minds of the eighteenth century: *Micromégas, Gulliver's Voyage to Lilliput.*

The first album of the *Prisons*, or, to translate their title more precisely, of the *Imaginary Prisons* (*Invenzioni Caprice di Carceri*), bears no date, but it is thought to have been published in 1745. Piranesi himself assigns them an earlier date in the catalogue of his works: "Plates produced in 1742"; the artist would have been twenty-two at the time. Thus these fourteen plates of the first *Imaginary Prisons* are just about contemporary with two youthful works, *Prima parte di Architettura* and *Opere varie di Architettura*, in which Piranesi draws certain fictive edifices with cunningly complicated perspectives, virtuoso pieces almost obligatory for artists trained in the Baroque tradition, and among which already figures the isolated image of a *Dark Prison*. They closely follow the publication of Giuseppi Bibbiena's architectural fantasies, *Architettura e Prospettiva*, which appeared in Augsburg in 1740. Their completion, or their first revision, is set around the period of the 1744 stay in Venice, when Piranesi is supposed to have worked under Tiepolo, another magician of theatrical architecture. But these images, which in many aspects refer to a fashionable genre, deliberately depart from it by their intensity, their strangeness, their violence—as if struck by the rays of a black sun. If, as is asserted, the delirious *Prisons* were created in a fit of fever, the Campagna's paludism favored Piranesi's genius by momentarily releasing certain elements which might have been repressed to the last, merely hinted at in his work.

We must define the word *delirium*. Supposing his legendary malaria of 1742 to be authentic, fever did not open for Piranesi the doors to a world of mental confusion, but to realms dangerously vaster and more complex than the one the young engraver had hitherto lived in, though composed after all of virtually identical materials. It increased the artist's perception to the point of erethism, and almost to torment, thereby making possible on one hand the dizzying energy, the mathematical intoxication, and on the other the crisis of agoraphobia and claustrophobia combined, the anguish of captive space from which the *Prisons* certainly resulted. From this point of view, nothing could be more useful than to compare these *Imaginary Prisons* with one of the technically perfect but coldly linear plates of the *Prima parte di Architettura*, for instance, the academic *Project for a Temple*, dated 1743, which is contemporary with or even very slightly posterior to the first states of the *Prisons*. Extend these perspectives; raise this drum vault already disproportionately high; bathe these still-conventional edifices and these tiny inhabitants in an atmosphere of dreams; make the smoke from these classical urns rise up in a more disturbing coil; intensify and simplify each line; and what you achieve will differ little from these hallucinated *Prisons*. Which signifies, in short, that in the *Prisons* Piranesi's genius shows itself at work for the first time.

This unexpected series of fourteen plates and the gayer series of four decorative compositions, the *Grotesques* of 1744, are the only works in which Piranesi abandons himself to what he called his caprice, or to put it better, to his obsessions and to his hallucinations. Diverse as they may be, *Prisons* and *Grotesques* both record the first shock of the antique and the Roman on Piranesi the Venetian. The *Grotesques* combine in a charming rococo *potpourri* certain fragments of columns, broken bas-reliefs and skulls which remind us a little of the gracefully macabre ornaments on some seventeenth-century tombstones, and a little of the delicate skulls and skeletons of Alexandrian carving. The enormously lofty *Prisons*, for their part, offer an inverted image of Roman and Baroque grandeur reflected in the darkroom of his visionary mind. The somber fantasy which, later on, reabsorbed within the actual and the concrete, still steeps the *Roman Antiquities*, is in these youthful works in a free state and, so to speak, chemically pure. For the *Prisons* especially, we must remember that the creator of this extraordinary series was only twenty-two years old. If we could compare an artist of the Baroque era to a poet of the post-Romantic period, we might risk calling these *Prisons* of the young Piranesi the equivalent of the *Illuminations* of a Rimbaud who did not subsequently give up writing. Perhaps they were his *Season in Hell* as well.

These *Prisons*, which modern criticism hails as a crowning achievement, were in their own day, as we might expect, very mildly appreciated and not at all understood, and consequently seldom purchased. In 1761, *i.e.*, seventeen years after the series' publication in its first form, Piranesi, now forty, offered the public a second, greatly reworked edition (*Carceri d'Invenzioni di G. B. Piranesi*), one which now contained sixteen plates. At the same time, the word *Caprice*, which figured prominently in the frontispiece of the first state, disappeared from this definitive edition, by an omission perhaps significant, or perhaps due merely to the formal rehandling of the title page.

If we look closely, we see that Piranesi's other changes in the *Prisons* are almost all of two kinds: he has multiplied the crosshatchings, permitting more generous inking, has diminished the great bright spaces, has darkened and augmented the areas of shadow; almost everywhere, too, he has added wheels, pulleys, cranes, winches, and capstans to the mysterious machines sketched in the foreground or in the corners of the halls; details which certainly transform them into instruments of torture rather than seeming the mere engines of construction they might have been; the wheels and platforms now ominously bristle with nails; from a brazier paradoxically flaming at the edge of a gallery opening out into the void rise blackened stakes, vaguely suggesting tortures; in Plate IV of the second state, a huge dark St. Catherine's wheel has replaced the noble column which constituted the axis of the perspective; clusters of chains hanging along the walls have proliferated like those of some hateful vine. Further, Piranesi has added two new plates (II and V) to the series, more vehement and more crowded with architectural reminiscences than the others. Finally, he has suppressed the fourteenth and last sheet of the first album, where we saw, against an almost bright background, two characters descending the steps of a central staircase, while a tiny veiled figure, a kind of mysterious counterweight, appeared at the right in a secret stairwell. This masterpiece of strange grace, which seemed to prophesy a kind of finale, *avant la lettre*, to an ideal *Fidelio*, has been replaced by the image of a black cellar decorated with grimacing Roman busts and lugubrious inscriptions, emphasizing almost to excess that the place we are in is indeed a prison.

Among the many reasons an artist of genius may have for modifying his work, the most common one does not apply here. There can be no question of a labor still blemished by inexperience now rehandled by the creator who has since achieved mastery: nothing, on the contrary, equals or exceeds the virtuosity manifested in these second states, if it is not perhaps that of the first ones. The most we can say is that meanwhile Piranesi has studied Rembrandt further, for we know that he admired the Dutchman's engraved work and that it certainly influenced his own productions, typically Italian though they are. It is possible, of course, that Piranesi, like his entire century, was swept by the current which drew Baroque art toward what we call pre-Romanticism, and that he deliberately modified his work in the direction of the gothic novel. It is also possible that, for some other reason, the notion of crime and the idea of legal prosecution increasingly preoccupied the creator of the *Prisons*. But above all, let us not forget that the eighteenth-century artist was supposed to offer his public an organized discourse whose signification would be patent to all, and not the more or less indecipherable product of a subjective reverie. Everything in these *Prisons* suggests that Piranesi had attempted in a lucid state to rationalize images which had perhaps lost the manifest meaning they possessed in his delirium, to justify their title by adding to these transcendental dungeons and dizzying torture chambers some unimpeachable detail of real dungeons and actual tortures—in short, to replace on the level of concepts and comprehensible emotions of the waking state, darker but also less unexpected, what had initially been the prodigious hallucination of an architect, the dream of a builder drunk on pure volumes, pure space.

Taken together, either in the edition of 1761 or in an earlier state, what first strikes us is that the *Prisons* bear very little resemblance to traditional images of a prison. In every age, the nightmare of incarceration chiefly consists in *confinement*, in being shut up in a dungeon which already has the dimensions of a grave. *Tu in questa tomba* … It also involves physical misery, ordure, vermin, rats swarming in the darkness—all the hideous decor of the *in-pace* and the *oubliette* which so obsessed the Romantic imagination. To these lugubriously permanent characteristics, our age will add the cold functionalism of its model prisons, the sinister banality of concentration-camp barracks which conceal the modern forms of torture and death, the mocking hygiene of the shower rooms of Belsen, the image of human crowds penned in the abattoirs of the first half of the twentieth century and in those the future holds in store. We are far from that loathsome horror and that sordid hypocrisy with Piranesi's megalomaniac and sublime *Prisons*. The sight of ancient Rome's places of incarceration could not have inspired him: the dreadful Mamertine Prison, where victims of the Republic and of Caesar suffered their last agony, consists of no more than two superimposed black holes, the lower barely the height of a man; Jugurtha and Vercingetorix suffocated in this pit with no outlet but the sewer of the Cloaca Maxima. Nor was Piranesi reminded of the medieval jails of the Castel Sant'Angelo, though he might have retained certain elements of its internal structure from this ancient mausoleum of Hadrian, like its helical corridor or underground room with the tombs, in order to serve them up again, much modified, in some plates of the *Prisons*; and the "leads" or "wells" above and under the Ducal Palace in his native city, which could have haunted this Venetian when he was drawing imaginary jails, also belonged to that type of prison in which the captive stifles or freezes in a narrow space. The pictorial art of the past, and in particular old Italian religious paintings, to which this eighteenth-century man doubtless paid very little attention, offer the one variant of the iron cage or heavily barred cell, scarcely spacious enough for the saint to receive the angel who comes to prepare him for martyrdom or else to save him; it was in this constricted form that Raphael had represented St. Peter's prison in the Vatican *stanze*.

Most of Piranesi's commentators, seeking a point of departure for the delirious *Prisons*, refer, for want of better models, to a certain Daniel Marot, a French draftsman and engraver who worked in England and who in 1708 published a little series of prints, one of which, the *Prison of Amadis*, already heralds the extravagant style of Piranesian dungeons. But this thread is very slender; actually it appears that the two engravers set out to depict quite independently an imaginary or a real setting: a tragedy king enslaved by his usurper, an opera knight imprisoned by a magician might fill with the *bel canto* of his distress these dizzying palaces related to no real prison. For example, Act III, Scene I of Metastasio's *Artaxerxes*, written in 1730, supplies the following brief indications, which, given contemporary taste for *trompe l'oeil* and perspective in the grand manner, might have inspired a designer less concerned with verisimilitude than with splendid effects of shadow and mass: *Parte interna della Fortezza nella quale e ritenuto Arbace. Cancelli in prospetto. Picciola porta a destra, per la quale si ascende alla Reggia.* It is probably from a description of this kind that Piranesi embarked to attain a region in which reigns a more mysterious anguish than that of the theater, and which sometimes seems to translate that of the entire human condition.

Let us consider these *Prisons*, then, which with Goya's *Black Paintings* are one of the most secret works bequeathed us by a man of the eighteenth century. First of all, what we are shown here is a dream. No connoisseur of oneiric matters will hesitate a moment in the presence of these drawings evincing all the chief characteristics of the dream state: negation of time, incoherence of space, suggested levitation, intoxication of the impossible reconciled or transcended, terror closer to ecstasy than is assumed by those who analyze the visionary's creations from outside, absence of visible contact between the dream's parts or characters, and finally a fatal and necessary beauty. Next, and to give the Baudelairean formula its most concrete meaning, it is *a dream of stone*: powerfully hewn stone, set in place by human hands, constitutes virtually the sole substance of the *Prisons*, with an occasional wooden rafter, iron jack, or chain; contrary to the program of the *Views* and *Antiquities*, here stone, iron, and wood have ceased being elemental substances—they now become no more than a constituent part of the edifice with no relation to the life of things. Animal and plant are eliminated from these interiors where only human logic or human madness rules; no trace of moss touches these bare walls. The natural elements are absent or narrowly subjugated: earth appears nowhere, covered over by tiles or indestructible pavings; air does not circulate— no puff of wind, in Plate VIII, animates the frayed silk of the flags; a perfect immobility reigns in these great closed spaces. At the very bottom of Plate IX, a fountain rim on which a woman is leaning (and both figure and object seem to have come out of the *Views of Rome*) is the only sign of water's presence in this petrified world. In several plates, though, fire is present: smoke rises from a cauldron strangely set on the brink of the void at a cornice's jutting edge, suggesting an executioner's brazier or a magician's crucible. In reality, it seems that Piranesi chiefly delights in setting smoke's pale and shapeless ascent against the verticality of the stones. Nor does time move any more than air; the perpetual *chiaroscuro* excludes the very notion of the hour, and the dreadful solidity of the structure defies the erosion of the centuries. When Piranesi could not help introducing into these buildings a rotted beam or a noble patch of ancient wall, he sets it, like a precious jewel, in the midst of timeless masonry. Finally, this void is sonorous: each *Prison* is conceived as an enormous Ear of Dionysus. Just as in the *Antiquities* one heard the faint echo of an aeolian harp in the ruins, the rustling of the wind in the weeds and rushes, here the roused sense of hearing perceives a formidable silence in which the lightest footstep, the faintest sigh of the strange and diminutive strollers lost in these aerial galleries would echo from one end of the enormous structures to the other. Nowhere sheltered from sound, one is nowhere sheltered from sight either, in these hollow, apparently vacated chambers linked by stairs and gratings to other invisible chambers, and this sense of total exposure, total insecurity, perhaps contributes more than all else to making these fantastic palaces into prisons.

The major protagonist of the *Antiquities* is Time; the hero of the *Prisons* is Space. Discrepancies, deliberately warped perspectives also abound in Piranesi's Roman albums; he remained faithful to the method of the engraver able to reproduce the totality of a building or a site—its various aspects, which in reality the eye does not simultaneously perceive but which our memory unconsciously collects after the fact. Almost everywhere in his interior views of Roman basilicas, Piranesi seems to place himself, and to place us, at the entrance of the edifice he is drawing, as if we had just crossed its threshold with him. As a matter of fact, he has stepped back some hundred paces, mentally suppressing the façade rising behind us, a trick allowing him to include in his sketch the whole interior but dwarfing the figures in the foreground as if they were glimpsed in a middle distance, while those at the very back become simple dots in this universe of lines. The result of this trick of perspective is to increase further the already existing disproportion between human size and the man-made monument. The stretching or warping of the perspectives of streets and squares produces the same effect, distancing or removing structures which would hamper the view, majestically raising the *Fountain of Trevi* or the colossal statues of *Monte-Cavallo* into a space greater than that actually around them; this procedure has influenced all subsequent architects and urbanists. In the *Prisons*, these games played with space become the equivalent of what in an inspired novelist's work are the liberties taken with time.

The irrational world of the *Prisons* dizzies us not from its lack of measurements (for never was Piranesi more of a geometrician) but from the very multiplicity of calculations which we know to be exact and which bear on proportions which we know to be false. For these figures high on a gallery at the back of the hall to have such infinitesimal dimensions, this balcony, which is extended by other still more inaccessible cornices, would have to be separated from us by hours of walking, and this discrepancy, which suffices to prove that this somber palace is only a dream, fills us with an anguish analogous to that of an inchworm trying to measure the walls of a cathedral. Often the arch of a vault in the upper part of the image conceals the top steps of a staircase or the end of a ladder, suggesting heights still loftier than those of the steps and rungs visible; the hint of another staircase plunging lower than the level on which we are standing warns that this abyss is also to be extended beyond the plate's lower margin; the suggestion grows even more specific when a lantern hung almost on a level with the same margin confirms the hypothesis of invisible black depths below. Moreover, the artist succeeds in convincing us that this disproportionate hall is hermetically sealed, even on the face of the cube we never see because it is behind us. In the rare cases (Plates II, IV, and IX) where an inaccessible opening gives onto an exterior itself imprisoned by walls, this sort of *trompe l'oeil* merely aggravates the nightmare of closed space in the center of the image. The impossibility of discerning any overall plan adds another element to the discomfort inspired by the *Prisons*: we almost never have the impression of being in the main axis of the structure, but only on a vectorial branch; the preference of the Baroque for diagonal perspectives inevitably gives us the feeling we exist in an asymmetrical universe. But this world without a center is at the same time infinitely expansible. Behind these halls with their barred bull's-eyes, we suspect there are other halls just like them, deduced or deducible in every direction. The frail catwalks, the drawbridges in midair which almost everywhere double the galleries and the stone staircases, seem to correspond to the same desire to hurl into space all possible curves and parallels. This world closed over itself is mathematically infinite.

Contrary to all expectation, this disturbing architecture is discovered, upon study, to be formed of very concrete elements which Piranesi elsewhere reintroduces into his work under apparently more real but actually no less visionary aspects. These subterranean chambers resemble the ancient reservoirs of the *Emissarium of Lake Albano* or the *Cistern of Castel Gandolfo*; these trophies at the foot of the splendid staircases of Plate VIII suggest those of Marius on the ramp of the Capitol; these posts linked by chains derive from the façades and the courtyards of Roman palaces where they quite banally serve to keep out carriages; these staircases whose balusters, flight after flight, encage the abyss are, but on a nightmare scale, those which princes and prelates of Baroque Rome mounted and descended every day; this hemicycle glimpsed in Plate IV through an arch decorated with ancient bas-reliefs resembles—but in the way things "resemble" in dreams—the colonnade at St. Peter's; this complicated system of volutes and semicircular arches is but an exaggeration of the Baths of Caracalla or Diocletian; these bronze rings between the teeth of granite masks are there not so much to tether weak captives as to moor Caesar's galleys. The preoccupation with specifically Roman archaeological details ultimately imposes itself on us with grim insistence in the three plates added in 1761: these piled-up blocks at the brink of a yawning excavation, these reliefs populated by monstrous wild beasts, these busts glimpsed in a sepulchral half-light increasingly suggest that the architect's delirium has been supplemented by the residue of the antiquary's nightmares.

Similarly, the fantastic machines which so redoubtably embellish the *Prisons* are nothing other than old construction devices whose use has persisted to our own day, and which an engineer familiar with archaic equipment recognizes and identifies at first glance. The gibbet added to the second state of Plate IX is the corner brace supporting a pulley which has served from time immemorial to raise loads; the ladders evocative of hangings are actually mason's ladders which here and there, in the *Antiquities*, lean against the walls of Rome; the cylinder armed with long points is a winch; this trestle which Piranesi has cunningly bristled with nails is the kind carpenters use for sawing; this ominous pyramid of beams is a jack the artist himself has diagrammed in his *Method of raising large blocks of travertine and other marbles used in the construction of the tomb of Caecilia Metella*; those scaffolds are scaffoldings. The very real resemblance between a historical period's instruments of torture and its technical machinery has permitted Piranesi to suggest in the *Prisons* the executioner's omnipresence, and at the same time to maintain, at the foot of these already titanic walls, the sense of the incomplete and the temporary, exhausting symbols of the architect's forced labors. Piranesi determined early on to explain the presence of these dreadful machines by their use as implements of torture, since even in the *Dark Prison*, published in 1743 in the *Prima parte di Architettura*, and which the artist did not subsequently add to the *Prisons*, we find the following mention: *Carcere oscura con antenna pel suplizio de' malfattori*. As a matter of fact, nowhere in his works do we see a corpse hanging from these immense gibbets, like Félicien Rops's *Bell Ringer* dangling from his clapper. Even in the blackest second states of the *Prisons*, the rope of a pulley and the plumb line of a pendulum serve only to score with a curve and a magisterial stripe the abyss these walls enclose. The same is true of the gigantic wheels set up almost everywhere in the depths of the dungeons, and which we occasionally find in the *Antiquities of Rome*, reduced to the modest role of hydraulic wheels or capstans: no human being is crushed on their enormous rims.

In reality, and though commentators have deliberately emphasized the "extraordinary torments" to which so many prisoners would be subjected in the *Prisons*, we are on the contrary surprised by the relative infrequency and above all by the insignificance of these images of torture. At the margin of the enormous bull's-eye which paradoxically fills the upper part of Plate IX, tiny figures are whipping a minuscule prisoner lashed to a stake; an imp, detached from a St. Andrew's Cross, falls like an acrobat from a prodigious height; and these wavering silhouettes here play the same part as the little windswept bushes atop the walls in the *Antiquities*. In Plate XIII, two figures descending the steps are indubitably captives with bound hands; in one of the plates added in 1761 (II), deep in a gigantic trench like some gutted ruin of an ancient monument, two pygmies drag by the feet a huge prisoner, himself exactly like a toppled statue; idlers scattered around the brink of this latomia urge on the executioners, unless of course their gesticulations are addressed to a stonecutter who is chiseling a block a little lower down. Here and there, by dint of plumbing the remotest corners of the *Prisons*, the eye discerns other captives, other jailors. But these tiny images take up scarcely more room than the battles or death throes of insects. Only once (Plate x) has Piranesi represented very distinctly a group of men being tortured; a sculpturesque group of four or five titans attached to stakes, limp or prostrate at the top of an immense voussoir. They look something like a Christ or a Prometheus facing each other in identical figures, as in some dream images. Colossal, with no relation to the tiny humanity strolling along the cantilevers or climbing the stairs, they move us no more than the prisoner in the frontispiece—brother of Michelangelo's *Ignudi* and also of the boys in Carracci's ceiling painting—wearing his chain around his neck like a ribbon tied in a bow.

Like their kind in the *Antiquities*, the tiny inhabitants of the *Prisons* surprise us by their alacrity, which is indeed typical of the eighteenth century. Strollers, captives, or jailors, some of these pirouetting marionettes hold a wand which may be a pike but which looks more like the bow of some shrill stringed instrument or a tumbler's balancing pole, and which here replaces the cattle prod the creator of the *Antiquities* likes to put in his rustics' hands. A suggestion of torment floats in the air of the *Prisons*, but is almost as vague as the suggestion of a sinister meeting with highwaymen in the *Views* of deserted stretches of the Campagna. The true horror of the *Prisons* is less in their few mysterious scenes of torture than in the indifference of these human ants roaming through enormous spaces, whose various groups seem almost never to communicate among themselves or even to take note of their respective presences, and still less to realize that in some dim corner a prisoner is being tortured. And perhaps the most singular feature of all this disturbing little multitude is everyone's immunity to vertigo. Sure-footed, at ease in these altitudes of delirium, such gnats do not seem to notice they are buzzing on the brink of the abyss.

But why has Piranesi given the *Imaginary Prisons* such characteristics, at once factitious and sublime, or, what comes down to the same question, why has he chosen to name these sumptuous architectural hallucinations *Prisons*? The influence of an illustration from a knightly romance produced nearly forty years earlier by a virtually unknown engraver, the hypothesis of a project for an opera decor of which not even the name has come down to us, are very inadequate explanations for the choice of this theme and this series of eighteen masterpieces.[2]

2   Eighteen, if we count, as well as the sixteen plates of the 1761 edition, the admirable Plate XIV of the first state, subsequently replaced by Plate XVI of the definitive edition, and the *Dark Prison* of the *Prima parte di Architettura*, which obviously belongs with the *Prisons* series.

Certainly the *Prisons* may well be one of the first and most mysterious symptoms of that obsession with torture and incarceration which increasingly possesses men's minds during the last decades of the eighteenth century. One thinks of Sade and of the dungeons of the Florentine villa in which his Mirsky imprisons his victims—not, as we have seen, that Piranesi heralds the cruel manias of the author of *Justine* as much as we might think, but because Sade and the Piranesi of the *Prisons* both express that abuse which is somehow the inevitable conclusion of the Baroque will to power. One thinks of Beccaria's argument against the atrocities of the prisons of the time, a plea soon to touch men's conscience and lay siege to the *Ancien Régime*'s bastilles. One thinks, above all, realizing the almost grotesque contrast between the poets' inner vision and history's anecdotal reality, that scarcely thirty years separate the fantastic *Prisons* from the very prosaic prisons of the Terror, and that the kindly Hubert Robert, Piranesi's friend and follower, would soon have occasion to paint, in the sordid bourgeois comfort of the Conciergerie, Camille Desmoulins waiting for his execution between a straw pallet and a chamber pot, an inkstand and a miniature of his Lucile. But despite the Promethean group of captives of Plate x, despite a gesture of pity or terror which the tiny characters sometimes seem to be making in the darkness, it is by no means certain that Piranesi himself was touched by the onset of horror and pre-Revolutionary revolt which his *Prisons*, in spite of everything, portend.

In the last plate of the second state, the somber incomplete inscriptions: *Infamos ... Ad terrorem increscen ... Audacias ... Impietati et malis artibus ...* suggest that the author sides with public punishment, with Roman law and order, and make out the prisoners of the *Prisons* to be malefactors rather than martyrs.

If we cannot account for them as an anticipation of Sade or the excesses of the Revolution, perhaps we should seek the secret of the *Prisons* in a concept which especially preoccupied Italian imaginations and which has always been fruitful in masterpieces—that of the Last Judgment, of Hell, of the *Dies Irae*. Despite the total absence of any religious atmosphere in the *Prisons*' formulation, these black abysses and these lugubrious graffiti are nonetheless the sole and grandiose equivalent which Italian Baroque art has produced of Dante's terrible funnel and his *Lasciate ogni speranza ...* In his *History of Art*, Elie Faure noted in passing that the creator of the *Prisons* remained in the great tradition of Michelangelo's *Last Judgment*, and this is true even of the single point of view of the steep perspectives and the disposition of space, and truer still of the viewpoint of interior perspectives. Michelangelo's work, impregnated by Dantesque concepts, seems to have served as an intermediary between Piranesi's entirely secular *Prisons* and the old sacred conceptions of an Immanent Justice. No God, it is true, assigns the Damned their places down the stages of the abyss in the *Prisons*, but His very omission makes the image of man's excessive ambitions and his perpetual failure only all the more tragic. These sites of hard labor from which Time and the forms of living nature are eliminated, these sealed chambers which so readily become torture chambers, but in which most of the inhabitants seem perilously and obtusely at their ease, these abysses which are bottomless and yet without means of escape, are no ordinary prison: they are our Inferno, our Hell.

"Denmark's a prison," Hamlet says. "Then is the world one," retorts dull Rosencrantz, for once foiling the black-clad prince. Are we to suppose Piranesi had a conception of the same sort, the distinct vision of a universe of prisoners? For ourselves, darkened by two more centuries of human strife, we recognize only too well this limited yet infinite world in which tiny and obsessive phantoms writhe; we recognize the minds of man. We cannot help thinking of our theories, our systems, our magnificent and futile mental constructions in whose corners some victim can always be found crouching. If these *Prisons*, for so long relatively neglected, now attract the attention of a modern public as they do, it is perhaps not only, as Aldous Huxley has said, because this masterpiece of architectural counterpoint prefigures certain conceptions of abstract art but above all because this world, factitious and yet grimly real, claustrophobic and yet megalomaniacal, cannot fail to remind us of the one in which modern humanity imprisons itself deeper every day, and whose mortal dangers we are beginning to recognize. Whatever the quasi-metaphysical implications of the *Prisons* (or, on the contrary, their total absence) might have meant for their author, there exists among the observations from Piranesi's own lips one sentence, uttered perhaps in jest, which indicates that he was not entirely ignorant of the demonic aspects of his own genius: "I have need of great ideas, and I believe that if I were commanded to design a new universe, I should have the folly to undertake such a thing." Once in his life, consciously or not, the artist kept that almost Archimedean pledge, which consists in drawing a series of diagrams of a world uniquely constructed by the power or the will of man: here is the result: the *Prisons*.

Like that of most artistic geniuses, Piranesi's glory has been intermittent and fragmentary, in that it has successively touched the various phases of his work. The *Views* and the *Antiquities of Rome* were immediately famous, especially outside Italy, where they initially met with less enthusiasm. One might say that they established forever a certain aspect of Rome at a certain moment of its history. They have done even more; since we possess, with regard to the periods preceding Piranesi's, no documentation equal in abundance and especially in beauty to his, and since furthermore we shall never know ancient Rome's physical aspect except through the cold and hypothetical reconstruction of archaeologists, the image Piranesi has left us of the Roman ruins of his day has gradually and retroactively extended in the human imagination; and it is almost mechanically of the ruins of Rome as Piranesi depicts them, and not of the monuments in their initial or older state, that we catch ourselves first thinking when we happen to name this or that Roman edifice.

Since the final years of the eighteenth century, there has probably nowhere been a student of architecture who has not been influenced by Piranesi's albums, and one can assert that from Copenhagen to Lisbon, from Petersburg to London, or even to the young state of Massachusetts, the buildings and urban perspectives drawn at this period and for the next fifty years would not have been what they are had their authors not leafed through the *Views of Rome*. Piranesi certainly counted for something in the obsession which ultimately swept Goethe to Italy, there to find a second youth, and Keats as well, who was to die there. Byron's Rome is Piranesian, Piranesian too Chateaubriand's and the more forgotten city of Madame de Staël, and the same is true of Stendhal's "city of tombs." At least until 1870 and the wave of building speculation which followed on the choice of Rome as the new kingdom's capital, the city's appearance remained Piranesian, and it is still in large measure the memory of this half-antique, half-Baroque Rome that irresistibly lures us today toward this increasingly transformed city.

While infecting the great public with a taste for ruins hitherto limited to a few artists and poets, Piranesi's influence has had the paradoxical result of modifying the ruins themselves. The longing to preserve and to restore, sometimes abusively, the ancient works of art greatly antedated the desire to preserve and restore the rubble from which they emerged. Until the development of this later poetry of archaeology, of which Piranesi's albums are one of the first signs, classical ruins, with few exceptions, had been regarded as mines from which to extract masterpieces subsequently added to papal or princely collections, or again, as Piranesi himself complained, as marble quarries exploited with a view to the erection of new monuments by popes eager to turn to Christianity's (and their own) glory what had been the pagan grandeur of Antiquity. These tragic and gutted ruins which Piranesi engraved, and the very circulation of his works, counts among the elements which have gradually changed the public's attitude, and finally that of the authorities themselves, and which have led us to the labeled, scrubbed, and replastered ruins of today, object of state solicitude and a national treasure of organized tourism.

The vogue of the *Views* and the *Antiquities* was substantially based not on an aesthetic or a technical merit few are competent to judge but on their subjects, which corresponded to the tastes of amateurs, acquainted since school-days with the names and sites of Roman history which constituted a part of the baggage of learning. With subsequent generations, such learning tended to shrink to little or nothing. Further, archaeological interest, strictly speaking, shifted for the most part to the monuments of hitherto inaccessible Greece, now restored to her European patrimony, then to a newly explored Egypt and the Middle East. Rome ceased to be that sole queen of the ancient world she had hitherto been, down to the end of the eighteenth century. Finally, these plates, admirable from so many points of view, suffered from the inflation sustained by the art of engraving in the nineteenth century and vanished into the inglorious host of images of famous sites or monuments, whose wide-margined, rosewood- or mahogany-framed examples embellish the dining rooms of so many provincial homes. Gradually Piranesi's *Antiquities* and *Views* passed with all the rest into an obscure corner of the hall or even of the attic. We come upon them there today with that entirely new and freshly motivated admiration we often experience in the presence of works which have outlived fashion and then that oblivion which follows fashion.

Piranesi's decorative albums, those drawings which, past Louis xv, Louis xvi, and the Directoire, anticipated Empire style, immediately found a certain echo in England, where the author had in 1757 become a member of the London Society of Antiquaries; they certainly contributed almost everywhere in Europe to the shift from Baroque to Neo-Classical. But in a more general sense, for this almost frenzied obsession with the antique to be imposed on the imagination of decorators and cabinetmakers, we had to wait until events had once again made fashionable Consular Rome and that of the Caesars, as well as forty centuries of pharaonic Egypt. It is curious to note, in particular, that the first germ of this so-called Egyptianizing style, with its profusion of sphinxes, Osirises, and mummies, is to be found not, as one might think, in the drawings of statues from the Nile Valley of Jomard's *Description of Egypt*, begun under Napoleon and completed under Louis XVIII, but in the Piranesian album of the *Arte d'adornare i cammini* of 1769, itself inspired by the modest pseudo-Egyptian statues found in the Villa Adriana between 1740 and 1748, and today in the Vatican.

The fate of the *Imaginary Prisons* was different from that of the rest of Piranesi's legacy. They were, as we have seen, somewhat overlooked in their own time, except by a few connoisseurs. In 1763, however, the *Prisons* figured in the library of Louis XV, and the accession memorandum praises their fine effects of light. Almost unknown to the great public during the nineteenth century, these structures created by the wand of a somber sorcerer were nonetheless to enchant several poets: Théophile Gautier said he would have liked to see *Hamlet* performed in a setting based on the *Prisons*, whereby he was at once very far behind and very much in advance of his century's notions of theatrical decoration. But it was above all Victor Hugo who seems to have undergone Piranesi's influence most profoundly, and allusions to the great Italian engraver are quite frequent in his works. It is obviously through the *Antiquities* and the *Views* that this man, who saw Rome only once in the course of his life, and then with the eyes of a very young child, imagined the city of the Caesars; it is likely that the "Ode to the Arc de Triomphe," with its evocation of the ruins of cities of the past and of the rubble of Paris to come, would not be what it is had not the author frequently leafed through those great images of Roman decrepitude. Hugo the poet (and perhaps, too, Hugo the draftsman) was haunted by the *Imaginary Prisons*. These "horrifying Babels Piranesi dreamed of" probably served as a backdrop to some of Hugo's poems; in them he recognized his own penchant for the superhuman and the mysterious. Here one visionary encountered another.

However, it is in England most of all that the *Prisons'* influence seems to have worked most powerfully on the imaginations of certain poets and artists. Horace Walpole saw them as "chaotic and incoherent scenes where death sneers in the darkness," an appreciation in itself more melodramatic than exact, but these dark images seem to reappear in his novel *The Castle of Otranto*, published in 1764, *i.e.*, three years after the definitive edition of the *Prisons*, and set in an imaginary Italian dungeon. The fantastic William Beckford numbered among Piranesi's admirers, and the vast subterranean halls of his *Vathek*, published in 1786, perhaps show the trace of these smoky *Prisons*. Curiously, Walpole and Beckford, both masters of the gothic novel, were also both passionate builders, and their whimsical structures, rococo-Gothic in one case, Gothico-Moresque in the other, though without in any way imitating Piranesi's Baroque grand manner, nonetheless betray the same obsession with a subjective architecture. But the finest British text concerning Piranesi comes from neither of these *rich amateurs*—it occurs, rather, in De Quincey's *Confessions of an English Opium-Eater*, or rather, in De Quincey's recollections of Coleridge. Let us reread the passage.

Many years ago, when I was looking over Piranesi's *Antiquities of Rome*, Coleridge, then standing by, described to me a set of plates from that artist, called his "Dreams," and which record the scenery of his own visions during the delirium of a fever. Some of these (I describe only from memory of Coleridge's account) represent vast Gothic halls; on the floor of which stood mighty engines and machinery, wheels, cables, catapults, etc., expressive of enormous power put forth, or resistance overcome. Creeping along the sides of the walls, you perceived a staircase; and upon this, gasping his way upwards, was Piranesi himself. Follow the stairs a little farther, and you perceive them reaching an abrupt termination, without any balustrade, and allowing no step onwards to him who should reach the extremity, except into the depths below. Whatever is to become of poor Piranesi, at least you suppose that his labors must now in some way terminate. But raise your eyes, and behold a second flight of stairs still higher, on which again Piranesi is perceived, by this time standing on the very brink of the abyss. Once again elevate your eye, and a still more aerial flight of stairs is described, and there, again, is the delirious Piranesi, busy on his aspiring labors: and so on, until the unfinished stairs and the hopeless Piranesi both are lost in the upper gloom of the hall. With the same power of endless growth and self-reproduction did my architecture proceed in dreams.

What immediately strikes us in this admirable passage is first of all De Quincey's entire fidelity to the spirit of Piranesi's work and then his extraordinary infidelity to the letter. First of all, the title is erroneous, for the *Prisons* have never been called "Dreams"; and it is interesting to see the two poets dropping, so to speak, from the title pages—the pediments of these prodigious palaces—their appellation of *Prisons*. Then appears the image of Gothic vestibules, unconsciously introduced by the two great romantics into this specifically Roman architectural world. But above all, one would seek in the eighteen plates constituting the total series of the *Prisons* in vain for that delirious staircase continuing its ascent, occasionally interrupted by missing steps, and where one and the same figure, evidently Piranesi himself, reappears a little higher up each time on new steps separated from the preceding ones by the abyss. This representation, so characteristic of a certain type of obsessional dream, was either transmitted by Coleridge to De Quincey, or else De Quincey himself, who had never seen the *Prisons* album with his own eyes, inserted it after the fact into the description Coleridge gave him. One or the other poet was pardonably misled by the very nature of this strange series. As a matter of fact, the *Prisons* seem to belong to that type of semihypnotic work in which one might say that the figures have moved, vanished, or reappeared between two winks of an eye, and that the sites themselves have mysteriously changed. The *Carceri d'Invenzioni di G. B. Piranesi* thereby provoked, in the author of *Christabel* or else in the author of *Suspiria de Profundis*, the image of a symbolic staircase and a symbolic Piranesi, truer than true, emblems of their own ascent or of their own vertigo. Thus the dreams of men engender one another.

The history of Piranesi's plates deserves separate mention. Brought to Paris by Francesco Piranesi during the Revolutionary period, they passed into the hands of the publisher Firmin Didot, who later resold them to the Academy of St. Luke in Rome, where they remain to this day. Piranesi calculated he could pull a total of three thousand examples from each copper plate, a figure much higher than that of most of the engravers of the time, whose plates sometimes deteriorated after one hundred proofs. This astonishing resistance of the plates, which permitted the abundant circulation of Piranesi's work, was due to the admirable simplicity of his engraving methods. He worked as much as possible by parallel lines, and appeared parsimonious of crosshatchings, which tend to form a little eroded islet on the plate where ink gathers unduly in the course of many inkings. Despite this technical perfection, Piranesi's originals ultimately eroded from use, and are no longer utilizable today. In his own lifetime, he often re-engraved the crosshatchings, which tended to blur. This is what causes his latest impressions to be the blackest ones as well. It is important that we not forget this detail when we seek out psychological reasons for the darkening of the second states of the *Prisons*, although the necessity of such retouching must have been less evident in their case than for other more frequently reproduced works by the same artist. However this may be, it seems appropriate to conclude our study by these few technical details, which prove once again how much a modest concern for artisanal perfection contributed to the great virtuoso's disturbing masterpieces.

Mount Desert Island
1959–1961

Sistine

The Maestro said to me:

"Here is the boundary stone at the crossroads, some two miles from the Porta del Popolo. We are already so distant from the City that those who depart laden with memories have almost forgot Rome by the time they arrive here. For men's memory resembles those weary travelers who disencumber themselves of some useless baggage at each stop. So that they arrive naked, with their hands empty, at the place where they are to sleep, and on the day of the great awakening will be like infants who know nothing of yesterday. Gherardo, here is the boundary stone. The dust of the roads has blanched the few trees which stand in the Campagna like God's milestones; near here, there is a cypress tree whose roots are exposed, which has difficulty surviving. There is also an inn, where people go to drink. I imagine that wealthy, protected women come here on weekdays to give themselves to their lovers, and that on Sundays families of poor workingmen celebrate by taking a meal here. I imagine that, Gherardo, because it is the same everywhere.

"I shall not go any further, Gherardo. I shall not accompany you further, because my work is pressing and I am old. I am an old man, Gherardo. Sometimes, when you wish to be more tender than usual, you call me your father. But I have no children. I have never met a woman as beautiful as my figures in stone, a woman who could stay motionless for hours, without speaking, like some essential thing which has no need to act in order to be and which causes you to forget the passage of time because she is always there. A woman who allows herself to be looked at without smiling, without blushing, because she knows that beauty is a grave matter. The women in stone are chaster than the others, and above all more faithful; only they are sterile. There is no fissure where pleasure, death, or the seed of a child can enter into them, and that is why they are less fragile. Yet sometimes they break, and their entire beauty remains contained in each fragment, like God in all things; but nothing alien enters into them to make their hearts explode with joy. Imperfect beings become agitated and couple in order to complete themselves, but purely beautiful things are as solitary as the grief of man. Gherardo, I have no children. And I am well aware that most men do not really have sons: they have a Tito, or a Caio, or a Pietro, but that is not the same joy. If I had a son, he would not resemble the image I had formed of him before he came into existence. In the same way, the statues I make are different from those I had dreamt of at first. But God keeps for Himself the right to be the knowing creator.

"If you were my son, Gherardo, I would not love you more; I just would not have to ask myself why I loved you. All my life I have looked for answers to questions that perhaps have no answers; I have burrowed into marble as if truth could be found in the heart of stones, and I have spread colors over walls as if I were plastering chords of music onto too vast a silence. For everything keeps silence, even our soul—or else it is that we cannot hear.

"And so, you are departing. I am no longer young enough to attach importance to a separation, even if it is definitive. I know too well that the beings we love and who love us best are imperceptibly departing from us at every moment that passes. It is in this way that they part from themselves. You are sitting on this boundary stone, and you believe you are still here; but your being, already turned toward the future, no longer belongs to your life that was, and your absence has already begun. Oh, I know that all that is only an illusion like the rest, and that there is no future. Man, who invented time, then invented eternity for contrast; but the negation of time is as vain as time itself. There is no past or future, only a series of successive presents, a road perpetually destroyed and continued, upon which we all go forward. You are sitting down, Gherardo, but your feet are placed on the ground in front of you with a kind of restlessness, as if they were testing out some route. You are clothed in the garments of our era, which will seem hideous, or simply strange, when our era is past, because clothing is never anything more than a caricature of the body. I see you naked. I have the gift of seeing the radiance of the body through clothing, in the same way, I suppose, that saints see into souls. It is a torture when they are ugly; when they are beautiful, it is another sort of torture. You are beautiful, with that fragile beauty that life and time lay siege to on every side and will finally take from you;

but for this moment it is yours, and yours it will remain on the vault of the church where I have painted your image. Even if one day your mirror gives you back nothing more than a deformed portrait in which you do not have the courage to recognize yourself, there will always be, somewhere, an unchanging reflection which will resemble you. In the same way, I shall fix your soul.

"You no longer love me. If you consent to listen to me for this hour, it is because one is indulgent toward those one is abandoning. You bound me to you, and now you are unbinding me. I do not blame you, Gherardo. A person's love is such an unexpected gift, and so little deserved, that we should always be surprised that it is not taken back sooner. I am not troubled by those you do not yet know but toward whom you are going and who perhaps await you: the person they will know will be different from the one I believed I knew and think I love. No one possesses anyone (even sinners cannot achieve that), and since art is the only true possession, it is less a matter of possessing than of re-creating a person. Do not misunderstand my tears, Gherardo: it is better that those we love should go while we are still able to weep for them. If you were to stay, perhaps your presence, superimposing itself, would weaken the image of that presence I want to preserve. Just as your clothing is but the envelope of your body, you are no longer anything for me but the envelope of that other person whom I have disengaged from you and who will live long after you. Gherardo, you are now more beautiful than yourself.

"One possesses for all eternity only the friends from whom one has parted."

TOMMAI DEI CAVALIERI

I am Tommai dei Cavalieri, a young lord, passionate about art. Handsome as I am, my soul is nevertheless even more beautiful, in such manner that my body, painted on the vault of a church, is nothing more than the geometric sign of rectitude and fidelity. I am sitting, my hand on my knee, in the pose of someone who rises with ease. The Maestro, who loves me, has painted, sketched, or sculpted me in all the postures life imprints on us, but I had sculpted myself before he did. What shall I do? To what god, hero, or woman shall I dedicate this masterpiece, myself?

What shall I do? Perfection is a road that leads only to solitude: I no longer see in men anything but surmounted rungs. The Maestro, who has greater genius than I, is in my presence nothing more than a poor man no longer in possession of himself, and Michelangelo would gladly exchange his ardor for my serenity. What shall I do? Have I sharpened my soul only to have a sword I shall not brandish? … That mad emperor wished that the world had only one head, so that he could cut it off. Would that it were only one body, that I might embrace it; one fruit, that I might pluck it; one enigma, which I might finally solve. Shall I seize an empire? Shall I construct a temple? Shall I write a poem, which will last longer? The parceling out of action disillusions me from acting, and each victory is nothing more than a broken mirror in which I cannot see myself whole. One has to have too many illusions to desire power, too much vanity to desire glory. Since I possess myself, what enrichment could the universe bring me—and happiness means nothing to me.

When men contemplate my picture, they will not ask who I was or what I did: they will praise me for having existed. I am seated on the capital of a column, as if at the top of the world, and am myself its crown. O life, vertiginous imminence! He for whom everything is possible does not need to attempt anything.

CECCHINO DEI BRACCHI

I, Michelangelo, dresser of stone, I have painted on this vault the image of a youth of Florence who was dear to me and is no more. He is sitting in a fierce attitude, and his crossed arms seem to hide his heart. But perhaps the dead have a secret they do not want you to know.

At first, I loved my dreams, because I knew nothing else. Then I loved my family (which was, as I think back on it, as if I loved myself) and the friends I acquired, who were laden with so much beauty that I was both humiliated and made happy by it. And, finally, I loved a woman. My parents are dead; my friends, my loved ones have departed: some have left me to live, others possibly for the betrayal of the tomb. I am not sure of those who remain; even if my suspicions are not justified, I suffer as much as if they were, because everything always takes place in the mind. The woman I loved, she, too, has departed from this world, like a stranger who discovers that she has come to the wrong door and that her own house is elsewhere. Hence, I went back to loving only my dreams, because nothing else was left to me. But dreams, too, can betray, and now I am alone.

We love because we are not able to endure being alone. For the same reason, we fear death. Whenever I have proclaimed aloud the love another being inspired in me, I have seen all around me the winking eyes and the shaking heads, as if those who heard me thought themselves my accomplices or permitted themselves to be my judges. Those who do not accuse you seek to excuse you, and that is even sadder. For example, I loved a woman. When I say that I have loved only one woman, I am not speaking about those others, those passersby, who are not women but only female flesh. I have loved only one woman, for whom I had no desire—and when I think back, I can't remember whether that was because she was not beautiful enough or because she was too beautiful. But people don't understand how beauty can be an obstacle, sating desire in advance. Even those we love do not understand that, or do not wish to. They are amazed; they suffer; they resign themselves. Then they die. Thus, we begin to fear that our renunciation has been a sin against ourselves, and our desire, lacking an outlet, having become as unreal and obsessive as a ghost, takes on the monstrous aspect of everything that has never existed. Of all man's regrets, perhaps the cruelest is that for the unachieved.

To love someone is not only to want that person to live; it is also to be astonished when he ceases to live, as if death were something unnatural. And yet, being is a more astonishing miracle than non-being; if you think about it, it is before the living that one must bow and kneel, as before an altar. I suppose nature gets tired of resisting nothingness, just as man tires of resisting the enticements of chaos. In my existence, which, as I grow older, is plunged into more and more crepuscular periods, I have continually seen the forms of perfect life strive to give way to others more simple, closer to primitive humility, in the way that mud is older than granite; and whoever carves statues only hastens, after all, the crumbling of mountains. The bronze of my father's tomb becomes coated with verdigris in the courtyard of a village church; the picture of that youth of Florence will begin to flake off the vault I have painted; the poems I wrote for the woman I loved will, in a few years, no longer be understood—and for poems, that is a form of death. The wish to immobilize life is the sculptor's damnation. It is in that respect, perhaps, that all my work is contrary to nature. At every instant, the marble in which we think we have preserved a form of perishable life returns to its place in nature, through erosion, patina, and the play of light and shadow over planes which thought they were abstract but are in fact only the surface of a stone. In the same way, no doubt the eternal mutability of the universe astonishes its Creator.

Before she was put into her coffin, I kissed the hand of the only woman who, for me, gave meaning to the whole of life; but I did not kiss her lips, and now I regret that, since her lips might have taught me something. Nor did I kiss the youth of Florence, neither his hands nor his pale face. Only, I do not regret that. He was too beautiful. He was perfect, like those whom nothing can touch; for the dead are all impassive. I have seen many dead. My father, having rejoined his ancestors, was no more than an anonymous Buonarroti; he had laid down the burden of being himself; he had effaced himself, in the humility of death, to the point of being no more than a name in a long series of men; his line no longer ended with him, but with me, his successor, for the dead are only the terms of a problem posed by each of their living continuers, one after another. The woman I loved, after the fatal illness which shook her as though it would uproot her soul, retained a hard, triumphant smile on her lips, as if, victorious over life, she silently despised her vanquished adversary; and I witnessed her pride in having crossed over into death. Cecchino dei Bracchi, my friend, was simply handsome. His beauty, which so many gestures and thoughts had, while he lived, fragmented into expressions or movements, became once more intact, absolute, eternal: one would have said that he had composed his body before leaving it. I saw smiles lift the corners of his bloodless lips, glimmer beneath his closed eyelids, and flood his face with the equivalent of light. The dead lie quiet, satisfied, knowing that nothing can destroy, since death cancels itself out even as it achieves its purpose. And because they have gone beyond knowledge, I have assumed that they understood.

But perhaps the dead do not understand that they understand.

FEBO DEL POGGIO

I am awakening. What did the others say? Dawn, you who reconstruct the world each morning; complete, with naked arms that hold the universe; youth, the dawn of man. What does it matter to me what others have said, thought, believed … I am Febo del Poggio, a scoundrel. Those who speak of me say that I have a base soul; but perhaps I have no soul at all. I exist in the way a piece of fruit exists, a glass of wine, a splendid tree. When winter comes, one abandons the tree that no longer offers shade; when one's hunger is sated, one throws away the pit; when the glass is empty, one takes another. I accept that. Summer, the lustral water of morning over lithe limbs; O joy, dew of the heart …

I am awakening. Before me, behind me, there is eternal night. For millions of ages I have slept; for millions of ages I shall sleep again … I have but one hour. Why would you spoil it with explanations or maxims? I stretch out in the sun, on the pillow of pleasure, in a morning that will never again return.

1931

That Mighty Sculptor, Time

On the day when a statue is finished, its life, in a certain sense, begins. The first phase, in which it has been brought, by means of the sculptor's efforts, out of the block of stone into human shape, is over; a second phase, stretching across the course of centuries, through alternating phases of adoration, admiration, love, hatred, and indifference, and successive degrees of erosion and attrition, will bit by bit return it to the state of unformed mineral mass out of which its sculptor had taken it.

It goes without saying that we do not possess a single Greek statue in the state in which its contemporaries knew it: we can barely discern, here and there on the hair of a Kore or a Kouros of the sixth century, the traces of reddish color, like palest henna, which attest to their pristine character of painted statues alive with the intense, almost terrifying life of mannequins and idols which also happen to be masterpieces of art. Those hard objects fashioned in imitation of the forms of organic life have, in their own way, undergone the equivalent of fatigue, age, and unhappiness. They have changed in the way time changes us. The maltreatment of Christians or barbarians, the conditions under which they have spent their centuries of abandonment underground until discovery has given them back to us, the sagacious or ill-advised restorations from which they have benefited or suffered, the accumulation of dirt and the true or false patina—everything, including the atmospheric conditions of the museums in which they are today imprisoned, leaves its mark on their bodies of metal or stone.

Some of these alterations are sublime. To that beauty imposed by the human brain, by an epoch, or by a particular form of society, they add an involuntary beauty, associated with the hazards of history, which is the result of natural causes and of time. Statues so thoroughly shattered that out of the debris a new work of art is born: a naked foot unforgettably resting on a stone; a candid hand; a bent knee which contains all the speed of the footrace; a torso which has no face to prevent us from loving it; a breast or genitals in which we recognize more fully than ever the form of a fruit or a flower; a profile in which beauty survives with a complete absence of human or divine anecdote; a bust with eroded features, halfway between a portrait and a death's-head. This blurred body is like a block of stone rough-hewn by the waves; that mutilated fragment hardly differs from a stone or a pebble washed up on some Aegean beach. Yet the expert does not hesitate: a line which is worn away, a curve which is lost here and reemerges there can only result from a human hand, a Greek hand, which labored in one specific spot during one specific century. The entire man is there—his intelligent collaboration with the universe, his struggle against it, and that final defeat in which the mind and the matter which supported him perish almost at the same time. What he intended affirms itself forever in the ruin of things.

Those statues which have been exposed to the sea-wind have the whiteness and porosity of a crumbling block of salt; others, like the lions of Delos, have ceased to be animal effigies and have become blanched fossils, bones in the sunlight at the edge of the sea. The gods of the Parthenon, affected by the atmosphere of London, little by little are turning into cadavers and ghosts. The statues reconstituted and repatinated by eighteenth-century restorers, made to harmonize with the shimmering parquets and polished mirrors of papal or princely palaces, have an air of pomp and elegance which is not antique but evocative, rather, of the festivities at which they were present, marble gods retouched according to the taste of the period standing side by side with ephemeral gods of flesh. Even their fig leaves clothe them like the dress of that time. Lesser works which people have not taken the trouble to shelter in galleries or in pavilions made for them, quietly abandoned beneath a plane tree or beside a fountain, ultimately acquire the majesty or the languor of a tree or a plant: that shaggy faun is a moss-covered tree trunk; this bending nymph is indistinguishable from the woodbine that embraces her.

Still others owe their beauty to human violence: the push toppling them from their pedestals or the iconoclast's hammer has made them what they are. The classical work of art is thus infused with pathos; the mutilated gods have the air of martyrs. Sometimes, the erosion of the elements and the brutality of man unite to create an unwonted appearance which belongs to no school or time: headless and armless, separated from her recently discovered hand, worn away by all the squalls of the Sporades, the Victory of Samothrace has become not so much woman as pure sea-wind and sky. One bogus aspect of modern art comes from these involuntary transformations of ancient art: the Psyche in the Museo Nazionale of Naples with her skull cut cleanly off, horizontally cloven, has the appearance of a Rodin; a decapitated torso turning on its base recalls a Despiau or a Maillol. What our sculptors today imitate by willful abstraction, and, moreover, with the help of cunning artifice, is there intimately bound to the fate of the statue itself. Each wound helps us to reconstruct a crime and sometimes even to discover its causes.

That emperor's face received a hammer blow on a certain day of revolt or was rechiseled to serve for his successor. A rock thrown by a Christian castrated that god or broke his nose. Out of greed, someone extracted the eyes of precious stone from this divine head, thus leaving it with the cast of a blind man. A German mercenary boasted that he had tumbled that colossus with one shove of his shoulders during a night of pillage. Sometimes the Barbarians are responsible, sometimes the Crusaders, sometimes the Turks; sometimes the lansquenets of Charles v and sometimes the soldiers of Napoleon; and Stendhal was later moved to tears at the sight of the Hermaphrodite with a broken foot. A world of violence turns about these calm forms.

Our ancestors restored statues; we remove from them their false noses and prosthetic devices; our descendants will, in turn, no doubt do something else. Our present attitude represents both a gain and a loss. The need to refashion a complete statue with artificial members resulted in part from the naïve desire to possess and exhibit an object in perfect condition, which is inherent to all ages because of the simple vanity of the owners. But that taste for excessive restoration which all great collectors from the time of the Renaissance down to our own day have possessed surely arises from profounder causes than ignorance, convention, and the vulgar bias in favor of a fair copy. Our forebears—perhaps more human than we and with different sensibilities, at least in the domain of art, from which they hardly demanded more than pleasurable sensations—found it hard to put up with mutilated masterpieces and with marks of violence and death on gods of stone. The great lovers of antiquities restored out of piety. Out of piety, we undo what they did. But possibly we are more accustomed to ruins and wounds. We are suspicious of any continuity of taste or of human spirit which would permit Thorvaldsen to repair Praxiteles. We more easily accept that this beauty, so remote from us and lodged in museums rather than in our homes, should be a dead beauty or a beauty made of fragments. And, finally, our sense of the pathetic is gratified by these bruises; our predilection for abstract art causes us to like those lacunae and fractures which tend to neutralize the forceful human element in this statuary. Of all the changes caused by time, none affects statues more than the shifts of taste in their admirers.

A form of transformation more striking than any other is that undergone by statues which have fallen to the bottom of the sea. The vessels which carried work commissioned from a sculptor from one port to another, the galleys into which the Roman conquerors crammed their Greek loot to transport it to Rome, or else to take it along with them to Constantinople when Rome became less sure, sometimes went down with all hands. Some of those shipwrecked bronzes, fished up in good condition like a drowned man revived in time, have acquired from their subaqueous sojourn nothing more than a beautiful greenish patina—as, for example, the Ephebe of Marathon or those two powerful athletes from Erice found recently. Fragile marble statues, on the other hand, emerge gnawed or eaten away, corroded, decorated with baroque volutes sculpted by the caprice of the tides, or encrusted with shells like those boxes we bought at the seaside in our childhood. The forms and gestures the sculptor gave them proved to be only a brief episode between their incalculable duration as rock in the bosom of the mountain and their long existence as stone lying at the bottom of the sea. They have passed through this decomposition without pain, through this loss without death, through this survival without resurrection, as does all matter freed to obey its own laws. They no longer belong to us. Like that corpse in the most beautiful and haunting of Shakespeare's songs, they have suffered a sea-change into something rich and strange. That Neptune, a good

workshop copy intended to decorate the quay of a small
town whose fishermen would offer him their first catch,
has descended now to the realm of Neptune. This Ce-
lestial Venus, or Venus of the Crossways, has become
the Aphrodite of the Sea.

1954/1982

On a Dream of Dürer's

One is unlikely to come upon many authentic dreams in
texts from another time; I mean dreams that the dreamer
himself has hastily noted down upon awakening. Some
splendid dreams recorded by Leonardo in his *Notebooks*
bear a curious resemblance to his drawings and paintings, but they give rather the impression of some oneiric experience extended into the state of waking or half-
waking than of a dream properly speaking. The poignant
dreams of Dante in the *Vita Nuova* and the great alle-
gorical dreams of Cardano are also located within this
intermediary zone—between dream, dream perceived
upon awakening, and *visio intellectualis*—experienced by
numerous poets, painters, and philosophers from the
Middle Ages to the Renaissance, but into which modern
man rarely ventures or, when he does stray into it, does
so unprepared and without a guide.

Yet we possess from a man of the sixteenth century
the extraordinary account of a dream which is nothing
but a dream, and, what is more, accompanied by a supporting sketch. It is found in Dürer's *Journal*. Here is
the account the artist, scarcely awakened, has left of
his dream:

*In the night between Wednesday and Thursday after Pen-
tecost [June 7–8, 1525], I saw in a dream what this sketch
displays: a number of waterspouts falling from the sky. The
first struck the earth some four leagues off: the blow and its
noise were terrifying, and the entire region was inundated.
I was so frightened I woke up. Then other waterspouts fell in
appalling violence and number, some striking the earth farther off, some nearer. And they fell from such a height that*

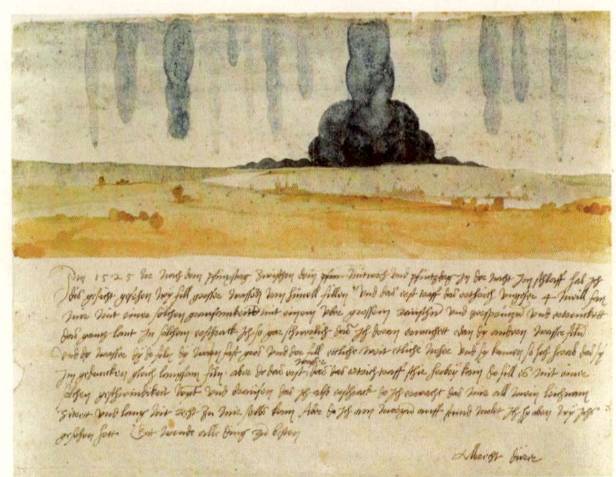

Albrecht Dürer, *Dream Vision*

they all seemed to fall in slow motion. But when the first wa-
terspout was close to the earth, its fall became so rapid and
was accompanied by such a noise and such a roaring wind
that I woke up, trembling in every limb, and took a long time
to get over it. So that, once I had arisen, I painted the above
picture. God makes everything turn out for the best.

This dream is striking for its complete lack of symbols. A German critic sees in it the effect on Dürer of the upheaval caused by the Reformation; but that's his theory. A psychoanalyst would suppose that the great painter was obsessed by water; but that remains to be proved. Water is not very dominant in the paintings and engravings of Dürer, and when it does appear, it is never catastrophic. One thinks of the peaceful Inn, with its limpidity that fills us today with nostalgia, in which the walls of Innsbruck are reflected, or of the calm Adige lapping the walls of Trent, or of that darker, almost fiercely solitary pond in a clearing which also possesses an imperturbable tranquility. Not only is the image of violent water almost totally absent from his work, but even this inundation seen in a dream doesn't at all correspond to the biblical sort of *Flood* in which mankind's fear and despair dramatically predominate. The sole rain which falls in his *Apocalypse*, engraved some fifteen years earlier, consists of huge drops of water falling from a cloud in which there appears a dragon with a lamb's head, and this is a minor detail. What is surprising, moreover, is how little cosmic these images from the Book of

Revelation are in Dürer, and perhaps also in Saint John before him, despite the showers of stars, the flames, and the clouds—which are symbolic configurations of the merely human drama.

In his oneiric sketch, on the contrary, the visionary is a realist, and it is of a cosmic drama that he is the spectator. He has the precision of a physicist. At the shock of the first waterspout, he tried to measure how far away he was from the point of impact, and then to judge the others in comparison with it. He noted the apparent slowness, then the accelerating, dizzying speed of these downpourings from far above. What is rare in a dream, so far as I am aware, is that he *felt* the percussive impact and *heard* the thunder of the falling water. One curious detail is that he says he was awakened by the shock of the first cataract, leaving us uncertain as to whether this awakening was part of his dream or whether he fell back asleep at once and was plunged again into the same cataclysm. In either case, the effect is one of a natural disaster perceived without reference to any human concept as it might have been refracted in a block of crystal without any human eye's beholding it. The terror which shakes the sleeper is, to be sure, a human reaction, yet an animal might just as well have experienced it, and this physical perturbation is very similar to that of an earthquake.

Look closely at the sketch, or rather the wash drawing, which depicts this dream. The enormous waterspout like a mass of blue-black clouds involuntarily makes us think today of an atomic mushroom; but we must reject such an overly facile prefiguration. The landscape seems crushed in advance by the dirty blue floods that fall vertically from the sky; the earth and the water which has already fallen are mixed together in a muddy brown and a murky gray: if one were obliged to identify this place with some spot on earth, one would think of the Lombard plain—which Dürer crossed more than once—because of the few scattered trees which are vaguely present in that atmosphere of catastrophe yet which one feels were planted and perhaps pollarded by the hand of man. Far off, made small by the distance, hardly perceptible at first glance, some brownish structures huddle on the edge of a bay, apparently ready to turn back into clay. What is about to be destroyed is not especially beautiful.

I repeat: there is no religious symbol in the margin, no avenging angels signifying God's wrath, no alchemical symbol of the "forces which descend," which would be pointless in the presence of the terrible gravitation of the cataracts. Nor is there any humanistic meditation, tragic as in Michelangelo or melancholy as it will be in Poussin, in the face of our greatness and smallness when confronted with the raging universe. Unless, perhaps, the best aspects of humanism are contained within this capacity, even in a dream and at the heart of a kind of ontological anguish, to persist in taking the measure of things.

The narrative itself ends on a pious formula, placed there by a man awakened from his dream. It reminds us, had we been tempted to forget, that Dürer was a Christian—twice a Christian, as it were, inasmuch as he was the heir and sublime interpreter of medieval piety on the one hand, and a citizen of Nuremberg, on the other, who at the end of his life hailed the Reformation. It can be variously interpreted as a quasi-mechanical propitiatory formula, as the more or less sincere assertion of an optimism based on divine benevolence (as inconclusive as some casual sign of the cross), or, on the contrary, as a very conscious submission to the order of things, which is always characteristic of every authentically religious great spirit. Marcus Aurelius accepting what the universe wills, Lao-tse in harmony with the void and Confucius with Heaven. But to say "on the contrary" is too much. We imagine that simple faith and impersonal adherence are somehow joined within those depths of human nature where the principle of contradiction does not enter. As such, this Christian mantra no doubt helped Dürer to emerge unscathed from his dreadful dream.

1977

Tone and Language in the Historical Novel

It has not been sufficiently emphasized that although we possess an enormous mass of written documents, and also visual documents, from the past, nothing is left to us of *voices* before the first nasal-sounding phonograph records of the nineteenth century. What is more, as far as the representation of speech is concerned, nothing, or virtually nothing, was achieved before certain great novelists or dramatists of the nineteenth century. By that, I mean that they were the first to register *conversation* in all its spontaneity, its disjointed logic, its complex byways, its lacunae, and its unarticulated implications without passing through tragic or comic stylization or lyric outburst.

Neither antiquity nor any of the intervening centuries offers us the equivalent of a conversation between Pierre Bezukhov and Prince Andrei in Tolstoy, between Ibsen's Rosmer and Rebecca West and her wily brother-in-law, or—at opposite ends of the spectrum—Vautrin's words as he propounds his views on life to Lucien, or the brief interchange between Marcel and the doctor who comes to listen to his grandmother's heartbeat. The transcription of speech in terms of pure realism, without any sort of bias, is curiously contemporaneous with those two mechanical means of reproducing the object as it is, the phonograph and the photograph.

Mutatis mutandis, the same observations can be made about the unspoken words which take shape within us under the sudden impact of an experience—Rastignac's impressions as he looks out over Paris from the heights of Père-Lachaise, the last thoughts that cross Anna Karenina's mind, the feelings of Prince Andrei as he lies wounded on the battlefield at Austerlitz. It follows that, for every novelistic attempt at re-creation, the representation of these various *unstylized* forms of speech constitutes an enormous stumbling block. One may indeed wonder if the methods used to achieve this in the novel as it developed in Europe in the nineteenth and the beginning of the twentieth century aren't really meaningless when applied to an earlier period. One may especially wonder if the fact that the ancients themselves have left nothing of this sort doesn't prove that the form of the novel is badly adapted to evoking ancient sensibility.

Let us look again at those literary texts out of which emerge, so to speak, the sounds and spoken rhythms of that period which extends roughly from Pericles to Julian the Apostate, a period of about eight centuries. The philosophical dialogue was a Greek genre par excellence, subsequently a Latin one by imitation: in it, literary conventions are, naturally, combined with dialectic conventions. It is only here and there, in brief passages (mostly in prologues or epilogues) meant to give the reader a rest, that Plato, with an admirable artistry (and I underscore the word *artistry*), slips in some short exchanges which might be those of contemporary conversation. The great tragedians, by definition, use a tragic style, itself often derived from the archaic terms and turns of phrase of epic language. The dialogues of comedy are often confined either to the language of humble people (one could write an entire essay on the amused condescension of comic authors in every era who reproduce, each in his own way, popular speech) or, more rarely, to the parody of polished language, such as the public believes is spoken. The utterances of Socrates in *The Clouds* are like the arguments of Bergson or Gabriel Marcel translated into popular jokes. Menander and Terence give their characters a language of bourgeois correctness, somewhat colorless, which was later imitated everywhere by the "high comedy" of the seventeenth and eighteenth centuries—a language which has never been spoken outside of the theater. The mimes offer us observations of an exquisite realistic precision, but, once again, based on ironic condescension: Herondas and Theocritus look down on their panders and gossips from a great height. The picaresque novel, of which we have only two examples, Petronius and Apuleius, sometimes has the limitations of mime, sometimes those of a "good joke" or popular tale.

Certain elegiac or lyric poems tell us something about the tone of voice in which emotions were spoken, cried out, or sung. We feel that that cry of passion in Theocritus's *Sorceress* must have been uttered more or less in that way. Without doubt, even overly literary works like Ovid's *Art of Love* supply us with something of the tone of flirtatious conversations—all the more so as that sort of conversation is based on conventions. Here and there the Greek epigrammatists open clear vistas: six verses of

Callimachus sum up what an intellectual faced with suicide must have thought and therefore said; the foreign slave asking to be buried according to his native rites, in an epigram of Dioscorides, must have spoken almost like that. Yet, once again, we find that *decantation* which is the characteristic, in itself admirable, of ancient literature: the poet serves as a sort of filter. Satirists exaggerate by profession. Some of Martial's epigrams give us the tone of Roman gossip; the broadside of insults directed against Caesar by Catullus must have been mouthed by many of Pompey's partisans; yet these versified obscenities are still literature.

The historians also simplify and schematize, distancing themselves, if not from the deeds (and who has better described deeds than Thucydides?), at least from the hubbub of words surrounding those deeds. We know that they undertook to rewrite the debates they inserted into their work, in order to make them express what the orator might have or ought to have said. Even less do we hear the tumult of an assembly in their works; yet stenographic transcripts existed; but it would have been contrary to their concept of history to have reproduced them as they were. Their purpose is, in effect, exemplary, as it is with Plutarch or (in another sense and *a contrario*) with Tacitus; or else analytic, as it is with Thucydides and Polybius. It is rarely, if ever, the reality of an incident seized at the moment, and even less the reality of verbal exchange and voice. Suetonius gives us the written equivalent of those realistic Roman portrait busts of private citizens and statesmen; but from that series of traits of character or of manners scarcely a spoken word emerges, and never so much as a fragment of conversation. To be sure, from time to time a "historic utterance," whether authentic or not (and I would maintain that at this distance authenticity is of little importance), causes us to hear a voice almost always raised to the diapason of a cry, or else some decisive words which sum up a situation and are engraved, as it were, for the posterity of all time (*Tu quoque, Brute* … , *Qualis artifex pereo* … , *Alea jacta est* …). We hear them, so to speak, in a void, isolated from whatever words or cries preceded or followed them—the angry interjections of the conspirators as they fall on Julius Caesar, the terrified murmur of the poor women and faithful slaves around Nero, the excited conversations of the officers and men as they crossed the Rubicon with their leader. In the exceedingly mediocre *Life of Commodus* in the *Historia Augusta*, the decree condemning Commodus to the Scalae Gemoniae stuns us, because it makes us feel palpably the enormous surge of hatred that swept over the senators as they looked on the dead emperor. It is one of the rare cases where the rumbling of a mob can be heard across the centuries.

Happily, there are sub-literary documents (that which I've just cited is one of them) which haven't undergone the filtering or rearranging literature entails. Legal judgments or decrees, such as the senatorial warrants or decisions punishing with death participation in the Bacchanalia, which cause us brutally to experience the terror of the people inculpated; letters of private citizens which furnish us with the tone of a student apologizing for having wrecked the family chariot or of a soldier asking his family to send him a care package; the letters of Cicero and Pliny, more consciously belonging to the "epistolary genre," which tell us something about written communications in upper-class society; graffiti which contain the scrawled echo of the talk and shouts of the street. They are voices out of the past, some of them practically in their raw state, each of them giving us the faint shock of the unexpected; yet there is nothing in them that would have enabled me to re-create with even a minimum of plausibility an exchange about serious or urgent, subtle or complex matters, a conversation between Hadrian and Trajan, or Plotina, or Antinous, or with his legate Severus concerning the affairs of Judaea. Nothing, or virtually nothing, is left us of those inflections, those quarter tones, those articulated half smiles which yet can change everything.

I shall inflict only one example upon the reader: I caused Hadrian to report, in scarcely amplified form, an incident which is recounted in a few words in a chronicle: the emperor, ill, had asked a doctor for some poison, and the doctor killed himself in order not to have to refuse the request. At the outset, the novelist adds to this skeletal news item a few details she hopes are plausible: the emperor's sympathy for the young doctor ("I took pleasure in his intelligence, both daring and dreamy, and in the dark fire of those deep-set eyes"); the subterfuges used to persuade the chief doctor, Hermogenes, from whom the emperor could not hope for this ultimate help, to go spend the day in Rome, thus leaving the sick man in the care of his young assistant ("An excuse came for me to get rid of Hermogenes for several hours: he had to examine candidates for the chair of medicine which I had just founded at the Odeon"); the interview which, on Hadrian's part, ends in supplications ("I insisted; I made absolute demand; I employed every means to try to arouse his pity, or to corrupt him; he will be the last man whom I shall have implored"); the equivocal response of the doctor ("Finally won over, he promised me to go and seek the dose of poison. I awaited him in vain until evening. Late in the night I learned with horror that he had just been found dead in his laboratory, with a glass phial in his hands"). I believe the tone of this passage to be more or less correct. But suppose I had tried to present these actions and conversations directly? I know that I would have fallen into error, into melodrama or pastiche, or both. In this regard, popular literature alternates between the servile copying of a few ancient expressions known to everyone ("Full, I am full," says the drunken patrician in the old French operetta ... "Bear these winged words to Metella") and the homespun ingenuity of Technicolor scenarios ("Spartacus, I think I am going to have a baby"). Someone will say that Corneille in *Cinna*, Racine in *Britannicus*, and Shakespeare in *Julius Caesar* managed it all rather well. But that is, of course, because they possessed genius. It is also—and perhaps even more to the point—because they were not concerned with *tonal authenticity*.

Without having compiled the preceding catalogue, I chose to make Hadrian use a dignified form of speech (*oratio togata*). Different though they are from each other, and whether they are called *Commentaries*, *Meditations*, *Epistles*, *Treatises*, or *Discourses*, the greatest works of the Greek and Latin prose writers who come before or immediately after Hadrian all belong more or less within this category of sustained style, half narrative, half meditative, but always essentially *written*, from which immediate impressions and sensations are virtually excluded and from which any verbal exchange is ipso facto banished. Obviously, it was not a question here of imitating Caesar or Seneca, or even Marcus Aurelius, but of deriving from them a pattern, a rhythm, the equivalent of a piece of fabric which one subsequently drapes as one will over the nude model. The "style of the toga" would provide the emperor with that dignity without which we cannot imagine antiquity—wrongly, no doubt, yet also with some reason, for dignity was one of man's ideals down to the end of antiquity: as he lay dying, Caesar arranged the folds of his toga. This style allowed me to eliminate those minima which are proverbially eschewed by the praetor. The sounds of spoken exchanges fell away by themselves: there was no more question of Hadrian's recounting his conversation with Osroes than of Caesar's having thought to put in writing his discussion with Vercingetorix. Even better, the *oratio togata* allowed me to present Hadrian addressing—beyond his contemporaries and his adopted grandson—an ideal interlocutor, *Man himself*, who has been the enticing chimera for all civilizations down to our time. He thereby addresses us.

But to speak of an address is also to speak of monologue; and it was at that level that I finally found the voice. Possibly that observation has more significance for Hadrian than for us, since in that epoch a man reading alone, and no doubt *writing* alone, read or wrote *aloud*. In attempting to rediscover that voice through the deliberate form of an address, I used the little—but the diverse little—that is left from Hadrian himself. We possess no more than three lines of the *Memoirs* he dictated to or had composed by an amanuensis, which no doubt constituted only a very official résumé of his life. Nevertheless, the man who admits therein to having got drunk as a youth at Trajan's table in order to curry favor with him was surely not a man who shrouded everything in lies; the strategist who, in an address to his troops, described with a refined precision their movements on a day of maneuvers reveals the intellectual beneath the general-in-chief. I tried to synthesize a series of strict legal or administrative decrees emanating from the head of state with the casual, light verses of the great amateur who, although he preferred the most difficult poets, seems himself willingly to have turned to the popular poetry of his day when he wrote his own verse. I had to make the best use I could of three intimate letters which are perhaps authentic and which, even if they aren't, at least show how at that time people thought Hadrian expressed himself. One, gay and playful, to his mother-in-law; another, detached, to a brother-in-law who was also his secret enemy; the third, very dignified, to his successor. A few writings by contemporaries who were part of his circle also seem, at moments, to refract his voice. Arrian (if it is indeed he), addressing Hadrian in his *Periplus of the Black Sea*, gives an example of the tender allusions his familiars made to the emperor on the subject of the dead and deified Antinous. The folklore gathered more or less from everywhere by Phlegon, his secretary, shows us the topics, if not the tone, of the casual conversations at table and at the end of a day's journey. The list of administrative divisions of Antinoopolis, charged with religious and mystical significance, carries us back to the orders given in his own voice by Hadrian for the founding of that city.

But perhaps those rare *spoken words* embedded in the heavy dough of the chronicles helped me even more: the retorts, some of a military brusqueness, others of an Italian finesse; the curt, lofty remark of the husband admitting that he would have got divorced "had he been a private citizen"; the bitter reflections of the aged man who cites Virgil at the deathbed of his heir (*Tu Marcellus eris ... Purpureos spargam flores*) but refuses the dead man official honors and grieves above all for himself ("All that has already cost the state too much money ... I leaned against a crumbling wall"); the irritated complaint of the sick man ("The doctors have killed me!")

whose last motto was nonetheless *Patientia*. Very little to go on: bits of voice out of which to reconstitute an entire tone or timbre of voice, the way others reconstitute a broken statue out of fragments of marble. And someone may say that tone and timbre here are nothing other than temperament, comportment, or character traits. I would agree. If the language of our characters is so important, that is because it expresses or betrays them completely.

I don't flatter myself that I always succeeded. A passage that delights many readers, the almost lyric description of Hadrian's voyages with Antinous through Greece and Asia, seems to me now a piece of bravura, an aria which focuses on what I have Hadrian call the summit of his years of happiness. I still believe that the emperor, retrospectively calling up his memories, could have seen them that way, vividly colored like the large frescoes at Herculaneum, stylized like the bas-reliefs of his hunts on the medallions of the future Arch of Constantine. But I no longer believe that he would have recounted them in quite that fashion—or, if so, am I then to suppose that at that moment he would plunge into a sort of Propertian or Tibullan elegy, making use, as it were, of all the resources of literature? I don't hold the passage against him, or against myself. It is always difficult to recount a moment of happiness.

I had the opportunity to verify, as if with a touchstone, the authenticity of another passage. A professor asked his students to translate into Greek (I should like to be able to say *retranslate*) that page where the emperor describes the state of atony which overcame him after the death of Antinous. I attempted it as well. Immediately, the *addenda* in a more modern tone became as discernible as the plaster which joins two fragments of a statue. Let me cite the passage, putting in italics the part which, quite definitely, does not work: "The journey up the river continued, but my course lay on the Styx. In prisoners' camps on the banks of the Danube I had once seen wretches continually beating their heads against a wall *with a wild motion, both mad and tender*, endlessly repeating the same name. In the underground chambers of the Colosseum I had been shown lions pining away because the dog with which their keepers had accustomed them to live had been taken away. I tried to collect my thoughts: Antinous was dead ..." Eight words refused to be written in Greek; they could have been written a bit more easily in Latin, a language which already underscores emotions as ours does. But in which language had I imagined that Hadrian, who was bilingual, was dictating his *Memoirs* to me? No doubt, sometimes in Latin and sometimes in Greek—which gave me a certain freedom. Yet there are moments when, inadvertently, I caused him to speak the French of my day, and these eight words seem to me, as I reread them, to constitute one such moment. The reader will ask why I do not then remove them. Because the impression, if not the expression, seems authentic to me, and because I regard inexactitude a bit the way the emperor, in my opinion, regarded risk; that is: after all precautions have been taken, it is right to let inexactitude play its part, and even to welcome the enrichments it may bring us. On condition, of course, that that part should be as small as possible.

Before leaving the emperor, I should like to protest against an adjective I too often see affixed to the title *Memoirs of Hadrian* in articles that are otherwise full of praise—*apocryphal. Apocryphal* is used, or should only be used, for what is false and tries to pass as true. The ballads of Ossian composed by Macpherson were apocryphal because they pretended to be by Ossian. Fraud is implicit in the word. My observation is neither irritable nor, it seems to me, trifling: that improper adjective (it would be better to speak of *Imaginary Memoirs*) indicates how little critics, and the public, are accustomed to the passionate reconstitution, at once detailed and free, of a moment or a man out of the past.

*
* *

The Abyss is polyphonic rather than monodic. It contains many conversations, from brief exchanges of a practical nature—yet inevitably charged with some emotional potential—to meandering dialogues where two interlocutors in agreement, or in partial disagreement, pass an idea back and forth between them in perfect trust, or, on the contrary, through double and triple layers of dissembled thought. Unlike *Memoirs of Hadrian*, the book is not written in the first person: that is to say, its world is not seen and described by one central character. In fact, just as I had felt early on that the tone of *Memoirs of Hadrian* would gain in accuracy from passing through the voice of the emperor, I quickly perceived that in *The Abyss* the contrast between the tone of voice of a modern narrator and that of characters from another century would be intolerable, and that the narrated parts should be done as much as possible in the indirect style, sometimes passing through Zeno himself or some other major or minor character, sometimes through "the voice of the people," as if through a muffled and almost always half-witted choral whispering. Life reconsidered by Hadrian from the perspective of memory gave way to life experienced from day to day at a level very close to the level of spoken language.

Up to a point, the literary style of the sixteenth century helped me with its concreteness and directness and a specificity it had inherited in part from one aspect of the Middle Ages. But verbal exchanges as such are as rare as they are in the literature of antiquity. The Latin dialogues of Erasmus are to the highest degree *written*. Those of Aretino furnish a mine of information about the low-life of his time, but they belong to the genre, which abounds everywhere, of the more or less satirical rendering of popular life. Italian comedy is highly stylized. The actual "words" reported by the chroniclers of the time mostly consist, as with the ancients, not of bits of conversation but of memorable phrases like that response (so fine because so immediate) made by the wife of the Admiral de Coligny to her husband, who had given her two weeks to make a dangerous decision: "The two weeks are already over, sir." ("My husband, the fortnight is already passed" from the mouth of Hilzonde in *The Abyss* echoes this, in a similar situation.) The same is true of the odious jokes uttered by the German Schopp at Bruno's execution, which I borrowed for Zeno's trial. Only Shakespeare and, here and there, his Elizabethan emulators give us—but a generation after the date when *The Abyss* ends—the lively tone of verbal exchanges in the sixteenth century, at least in those passages where a certain rhetoric hasn't smothered them. But that passionate rhetoric is itself characteristic of the time: some of the lyrical soliloquies of Lear or Hamlet, which audibly belong to the world of the theater, nonetheless tell us something about the language for emotions violently felt by certain especially strong or thoughtful people. They shed a light on the thinking, feeling men at the end of that century which we don't have again in the same intensity for any other era before our own.

There is a constant shifting between the written and the spoken in certain works of the sixteenth century. Not in all, of course: the humanists who copied antiquity destroyed scholastic routines of thought and expression, but only to create others, essentially oratorical, which have sometimes lasted down to our time. Those works we still read, in any case, are very close to the oral mode. When we read Montaigne, we often feel we are silently participating in a unilateral conversation; all the freshness and rudeness of common speech is in Luther. The exchange of indignant letters between Agrippa of Nettesheim and an honest curate of Metz on the subject of a scandalous Inquisition affair has all the heat of oral testimony. In the *Journal* which Dürer kept as a strictly personal memorandum and in more of a spoken than a written style, his notes on the death of his mother burst from the page in the midst of his financial accounts and descriptions of wayside lodgings, and we are haunted by the mixture of sketches and incomplete phrases he jotted down when he awoke from a nightmare.

Beyond such intimate works, we encounter the secret ones. Privately, in his mirror writing, Leonardo composed *Notebooks* which were for him alone; and the fact that they have appeared only by accident some three centuries later gives us the feeling of entering, unencumbered by any intermediary interpretation, into the very interior of a man of genius making a record of himself without any witnesses. They are unliterary notebooks, for Leonardo was even more of an autodidact than Zeno; yet they achieve the poetry of pure *tone*, like everything that comes directly from the self. Some of the secret reports of the ambassadors of Venice have the sound of a whispering voice. The soiled pages, in an Italian jargon besmirched with Latin, of the scribe who put down in writing the incoherent mumblings of Campanella when he was being subjected to torture, or those of the informer who noted down the words the philosopher exchanged with his friend Fra Pietro Ponzio in prison, seem even more literally slices of life, cries torn from a man thrashing about in anguish and the clandestine echo of a conversation that was already clandestine. In their time, they were shown only to the rather distracted or astute eyes of the judges; then they were buried in the judicial archives of the Kingdom of Naples until their publication in 1886. Yet it seems as though their specific horror has not evaporated in the slightest in the time between the actual event and now. In *The Abyss*, I made no use of the first of these documents, having spared Zeno torture in order to avoid any touch of melodrama; from the second I took only the affectionate Fra Pietro's *eamus ad dormiendum* and his *cor meum*, which Zeno hears murmured out of the depths of his past by the voice of another friend a quarter of an hour before his death. Yet no other piece of writing has ever so vividly brought me the *auditory* shock of the crumbling of the walls of time.

The fact that we still have an oral knowledge of the language, or rather the languages, that Zeno speaks (for if Hadrian is bilingual, Zeno is polyglot), which we shall never have of the Latin and Greek of the second century, contributed to this drift toward spoken language in *The Abyss*. Despite the fact that French changed, mostly for the worst and in the direction of a narrowing and constraining propriety, between about 1550 and the present, many of my characters' phrases would still have come into my mouth just as they were. At the risk of creating the impression of excessive meticulousness, I confess to having turned to dictionaries for every doubtful word—

that is, for each word which I suspected had entered the language after the sixteenth century or, at most, after the beginning of the seventeenth; and those words I ruthlessly suppressed because they carried with them ideas that my characters could not have had in that form. With almost equal care, I did my best to avoid as much as possible every word which had ceased to be in common usage after the end of the sixteenth century and which I might have been tempted to use out of a love for the picturesque or the archaic, with no other valid psychological reason. It is because of words or phrases inserted to give a sense of period that the "historical novel" disqualifies itself, as often as it does because of anachronisms.

Let me give a few examples. The word *Protestant* is used from time to time from the beginning of the sixteenth century, but it still wavers imperceptibly between its current meaning (a member of a Christian religion) and its meaning as an active participle (a man who protests); and subsequently it is laden for the reader with meanings that come from more recent stages of Protestantism. It is above all in its meaning of an armed faction that it is used in *The Abyss*, as is the word *Catholic* as well ("the Protestant princes," "our Catholics"). *Huguenot* is meaningful only against a French background, and the characters of this novel live mostly in the lands of the Holy Roman Empire; moreover, it is almost as aggressively archaic a word as *rapier*. The words *Lutherans*, *Calvinists*, and *Anabaptists*, which have a narrower focus, are more useful for our particular subject: they indicate to what degree these groups were still perceived as separate, sometimes violently divergent, not yet fused into an entity perceived from without as monolithic. The same observation applies to *Iconoclasts*, which sometimes designates Anabaptists, sometimes Calvinists, sometimes both, and which gives us nothing more than what the bourgeoisie of large Flemish towns deigned to know about some dangerous rebels. "Members of the supposedly Reformed Religion" is an adequate designation on the lips of ecclesiastics and jurists. When I looked into some of the translations of *The Abyss*, I discovered that Captain Henry Maximilian spoke of syphilis like a twentieth-century sociologist, instead of referring to the good old pox of the soldier; the fact that the learned word figures in a Latin allegory composed by a doctor of the period makes no difference, since it became a word of common usage only much later, and then initially as a euphemism. The word *bugger* suffered a good deal at the hands of some of my translators. Some prudishly rendered it as *heretic*, which wouldn't have been right except in the twelfth or thirteenth century; others made it into a sort of *good old chap*, much too modern, even though the word must have rapidly slipped into that sort of meaning. The sexual significance eluded them, even though it was present in the usage of the sixteenth and seventeenth centuries. *Patriot*, which acquires currency only in the eighteenth century, would have been ridiculous in popular speech around 1550, yet it's often found in the *Chronicles of the Troubles in the Low Countries*. Anticipating by at least two centuries, the literate bourgeoisie of those provinces, in their struggle against the hereditary ruler from Spain, in fact took it from their reading in Greek and Latin, adapting it in their own fashion. It was appropriate to the cultivated speech of the Prior of the Cordeliers ("My godson, Monsieur de Withem, one of the Patriots …"). The adjective *Belgic* is another word that caused me problems. Some readers who were not very *au courant* about the history of the language believed it was born around 1830, when, instead, it died, to be replaced by the word *Belgian*, and was rather awkwardly reincarnated in the proper name of a then new nation. Certain worn-out words can serve, like a nail, to fix a date, and their use is then legitimate: when Zeno emerges from his meditation on time and space and recalls that at that moment he is lying on a corner of Belgic soil, that adjective takes him back into the sixteenth century.

Ancient man, at least when he belonged to that small minority of cultivated minds which hides from us all the other, illiterate minds of the time, tended, on principle, to rationalize the irrational and to move from the particular and concrete to the general and essential. With certain specific exceptions, of course: in history, as I've already said, Suetonius; in art, the carvers of Roman portrait busts. The great minds of the sixteenth century, again with certain specific exceptions, individualize and particularize. One has only to compare an anecdote of Plutarch with its retelling by Montaigne to be convinced of this. The language of *The Abyss* was obliged to take account of this specificity in practically every line. The vocabulary of the sixteenth century is, happily, close enough to our own so that a specific word for the designation of a specific object only occasionally causes the modern reader a semantic shock. Had I wished to render every detail of every incident of Hadrian's life, I should have had cautiously to get round the words *triclinium*, *quadriga*, and *sella curulis*, partly to avoid any pedantry, but especially to leave antiquity its aspect of unencumbered space—which aspect is patently false, and yet at the same time is also partially true if one recalls that the Near East or even Italy has always tended toward a simple way of life, even in ostentation. In *The Abyss*, on the contrary, every word referring to an object, as well as the object itself, is often (for how much longer?) familiar enough to us to become, when Zeno's meditation demands it, suddenly *unfamiliar*—which an object or a word belonging to a civilization too far back from ours could not achieve. For the painters of the northern Renaissance, objects form a whole with the personage represented and, sometimes, overwhelming him, acquire a disquieting sort of life of their own; so also in *The Abyss*, the objects, and accordingly the words that designate them, become the expression of a certain rapport or the sign of a certain submission to necessity. Thus, to choose from among many examples: the bowl of soup that Zeno takes in the refectory of the convent after a sleepless night at the bedside of the prior, the blade less than two inches long which will open the way to death for him, and the nightshirt he uses to stuff up the space between the door and the floor of his prison so that the guard will not see blood on the floor of the corridor. Each precise word became a part of the conditioning of the characters, that conditioning which most of them submit to passively, but which some, like Zeno, explore and, to a certain extent, manage to rid themselves of, even at the cost of their lives.

What I've said about words designating deeds and things should also be said about words which characterize individuals. In *Memoirs of Hadrian*, even had the book been written in a "polyphonic" style (and this is a good reason why it wasn't), we would have heard almost no specific differences between the language of Arrian, Attianus, Chabrias, and Hadrian himself; the variants would be ones of temperament (the tone of Trajan, for example, would sometimes have had to be more jovial, sometimes more imperious than that of Hadrian); the intellectual orientations—Stoicism for one, Pythagoreanism for another, Pyrrhonism for a third—would at most have been perceived as subtle nuances: taken together, these intelligent men belong to an all-embracing culture and, at least at their level of society, speak more or less the same language. The tonal differences among the characters of *The Abyss* form a series of opposing angles—in part, to be sure, because time has not eroded to the same extent the conflict of their opinions, the consequences of which still affect us; in part, above all, because sixteen centuries of often badly formed thoughts, or thoughts that shouldn't have been formed at all, have dug indelible furrows into men's minds. Rightly or wrongly, the ancient world seems to us less scarred. The three ecclesiastics introduced into *The Abyss* do not speak the same language, and none of them *knows* completely, or at least doesn't *use* completely, that of Zeno. The philosopher and the canon appear to converse, yet almost none of the underlying ideas of the former reaches into the man of the Church, who is nevertheless judicious in his fashion; and nothing of the experience of the unfaithful monks really penetrates his legalistic and theological mind, even though he is their judge: they might just as well have lived in another time and another world. The bishop's impersonal tone is nothing other than that of the schools of his day: it teaches us nothing about the man. The very spontaneous language of the Prior exists on at least three levels: that of the former statesman who is well informed about public affairs; that of the director of conscience and the father superior, who is strict and austere; and that of the man of prayer. Zeno, with a clearly warranted prudence or a defiance of the Church the Prior represents (combined with a tenderness for who he *is*), sometimes feigns not to understand his poignant confidences; but it is no doubt also true that the profound plainsong of charity in the words of his pious protector eludes him, at least at first. In contrast, the Prior penetrates the mind of his interlocutor more than Zeno realizes, yet he voluntarily places a zone of silence between his friend's overly audacious thoughts and his own ("Pray do not insinuate a thing which I do not wish to hear"). The captain Henry Maximilian, a man with an open mind, who has had the experience of certain humanist teachings and is bound to Zeno by shared memories of childhood, *hears* the words the philosopher speaks; beyond a certain point, though, he no longer follows them. Princes and merchants confine themselves to their professional vocabulary of merchants and princes.

Zeno's language is made out of successive formations. The oldest is the Flemish of the street, the servants' hall, of the more or less clandestine encounters with workmen, which comes back to the surface during the last years he spends in Bruges. The French spoken in his home is already a language of culture; it is also the language of the books he writes and of his conversations with the Captain and the Prior of the Cordeliers. But the German, Italian, Spanish, and even Arabic from his years of wandering vie for position with this French. The Latin from his scholastic education unfailingly returns to his lips; if he thinks with these various tools of language, he reasons in Latin, or at least with the aid of the logical principles which come to him from that language: that is why I planted a bit of that Latin, which has no connections with that of the humanists, here and there in his talk, like so many signposts. The scientific language, with its mathematical metaphors as they would have been formulated in the seventeenth century, is clearly not yet his own; the language of experiments, which is his, also belongs to the artisans with whom he works and the sick people he takes care of, German in Lübeck, Flemish in Bruges. One of his distractions in prison will be to contrive an ideal language for himself which is free from any constraint except that of logic. In the chapter entitled "The Abyss," where he finds himself on the borders of the inarticulate and the ineffable, words and even concepts become silent; the differing states of consciousness are translated into the metaphors of alchemy, in which float all the recurrent myths of humanity.

I believe I came to this spontaneity of language, which is beyond thought or speech, only toward the end of the first section of the book. With very few exceptions (the most notable of which is perhaps the day spent by Zeno in the forest of Houthuist), the first hundred pages preserve the tone of a chronicle; the few conversations are composed of what the author assumes her characters would have said in those circumstances: they do not spontaneously flow from their lips. The account of the festivities at Dranoutre interrupted by the arrival of the weavers is composed contrapuntally, and each voice enters only for its appropriate part, too measured to be anything more than a sonorous tag. The conversation between Zeno and Vivine is written to the tune of a ballad, but it's hard for me to know whether that was because I was satisfied with that stylized form and that rather superficial level, or whether the young girl herself could not have spoken otherwise, or even the young Zeno, who surrenders to the game. In any case, it doesn't seem to me that complete freedom of language is achieved until the moment when Zeno, matured and already beginning to age, meets his comrade Henry Maximilian again at Innsbruck. From that moment until the end of the book, I had the impression I was a bit farther away from the reconstruction of life in the sixteenth century and a bit closer to that life itself.

1972

Official report of the trial of Campanella, 1597–1601

I. *Report of a spy*

A certain Francesco Tartaglia, detained for twelve days in the Castel Nuovo of Naples by order of the Royal Councilor, Don Giovanni Sánchez de Luna, several times heard Fra Tommaso Campanella and Fra Pietro Ponzio speaking with each other. In particular, on the night of April 14, Tartaglia and two prison guards, Martínez and Onofrio, heard the following:

Fra Pietro called four times to Fra Tommaso, saying:

Fra P.: O Fra Tommaso, Fra Tommaso, Fra Tommaso, O Tommaso, don't you hear me, my beloved friend?

Fra T.: Hello! Hello!

Fra P.: O, dear heart, how are you? Take courage, for the messenger is coming tomorrow, and we shall learn something.

Fra T.: O Fra Pietro, can't you arrange to get this door opened so that we can sleep together? That would be such happiness!

Fra P.: Would that God might make it possible for me to give the guards ten ducats and you, my beloved friend, ten kisses every hour! I distributed your sonnets throughout Naples, and I know them all by heart. There's nothing I'd rather do than read something of yours.

Fra T.: I plan to give some copies to the messenger.

Fra P.: Oh yes, dear heart, but do me the grace to give me some first, for me and my brother Ferrante, and then make some for the messenger.

Fra T.: Go to sleep now. Good night.

[*Signed*: Tartaglia]

[In another hand]

Fra T.: Have you any news of your little brother and your godfather?

Fra P.: They've put them with the laymen, with Gioseppo Grillo and Francesco Antonio Olivieri.

Fra T.: That's where your brother is?

Fra P.: Ferrante is with that bunch of laymen.

Fra T.: Oh, what a pity! Who knows what will become of poor little Francesco Antonio d'Oliviero …

Fra P.: Now you see … Have you written much today?

Fra T.: Yes, quite a bit.

Fra P.: Martínez isn't in the Castel, and the captain has called for Onofrio. We can speak freely.

Fra T.: You don't know the Spanish!

Fra P.: I know them well enough, *and* their crimes!

Fra T.: Do you know if Thomas Assarus is free?

Fra P.: I know nothing. Ask someone on the floor above.

Fra T.: That's not possible. Fra Pietro, tomorrow I'll try to slip you a note containing what I daren't say aloud. I hear someone.

Fra P.: God save us from them. Speak in Latin: they are
   ignorant and don't understand it.
[They are silent for a moment.]
Fra P.: There's no one. They wouldn't come without a
   torch.
Fra T.: Do you have any light?
Fra P.: No, none at all.
Fra T.: I see light. Let's go to sleep.
Fra P.: Let's go to sleep.

II. *Minutes of a torture session undergone by Campanella*

a) July 18, 1600

The accused: I feel terrible.
They tell him they are going to torture him again.
The same: Please, no! What do you want of me? I'm dead.
They ask him why he will not answer their questions.
The same: I can't … Aaaah, aaaah, aaaah! Assholes! My
   whole body hurts, brother … Let me down … Have
   you no pity?
They ask him why he does not tell the truth.
The same: I can't stand it anymore. Brother, I'm pissing.
   [And he begins to piss.]
For a while he is silent. Then he says:
The same: I'm shitting in my pants.
Then he is silent. They ask him to speak.
The same: I can't.

They tell him to beg the Lord Judges for mercy.
The same: Let me shit … My God, I'm dying!
They ask him if his dinner was good.
The same: I can't stand it anymore.
They ask him the name of the Commissioner of the Holy
Office who arrested him.
The same: Let me go to sleep, Fra Tommaso …
They ask him who Fra Tommaso is.
The same: Fra Tommaso is me.
They take him down and lead him back to prison.

b) Session of June 4–5, 1601, in the presence of two bish-
ops and an apostolic pronotary

They tell him he'll be cruelly treated if he continues to
play the fool.
He answers:
The accused: Ten white horses …
Several more impertinent answers. They tie him to the
rack.
The same: Tie me tight … You're crippling me. Aaaah!
    O my God!
They tell him to be reasonable.
The same: I've done nothing to you … Let me go, I'm a
    saint! … *Sanctus sum, miserere* … Aaaah! My God … I
    am dead, my dear heart! Dead! … Oh, they're tighten-
    ing my hands … Oh, I haven't done anything. Listen! …
And he continues to cry out, saying over and over:

The same: Aaaah!

And he suffers the torture, saying:

The same: Oh, where are the soldiers who helped me? …
Please come … Oh, I'm dying … Help me! … I'm
shitting …

They tell him not to play the fool.

The same: Let me go … Don't kill me … I'll give you a
dozen carlins … I've done nothing!

They tell him not to play the fool. Then, as they were
tying his feet, he said:

The same: Oh, they're killing me …

And when he hears the trumpet calls from the boats in
the port of Castel Nuovo, he says:

The same: Blow! Blow! They've killed me!

They tell him not to pretend, and he remains silent, his
head bent down over his chest, for an hour.

They tell him they will let him down if he agrees to talk,
but he says only:

The same: No … I'm pissing …

He asked to get down, and was let down, and said:

The same: I want to shit.

And they took him to the latrines. And then he was inter-
rogated again by the Lord Judges, and he says:

The same: My name is Friar Tommaso Campanella.

They ask him where he was born and how old he is. He
does not answer. The Lord Judges order him to be put
back on the rack. They put him back and arrange him
on it. He says:

The same: Oh, you're killing me!

They order him to answer and not go to sleep. He says:

The same: Please be seated … Please be seated … A
    chair … Be quiet … Be quiet …

They ask him where he was born and how old he is, and
he says:

The same: Help!

And he is silent.

They tell him to stop playing the fool, and he keeps silent.
He bows his head and says:

The same: Alas! Alas!

And when the first hour of the night had passed, they
again asked him where he was born and how old he was,
and he says to the Lord Judges:

The same: Don't do this! I am your brother!

And he is silent.

And they tell him not to play the fool, and he says:

The same: Give me something to drink!

And they give him a drink, and he shouts out:

The same: Help! … O joy!

And the second hour of the night passed, and they tell
him not to play the fool, and he says:

The same: Do not kill me, brother!

And they ask him if he is a priest or a layman, and he re-
plies with many impertinences, and says:

The same: I am a Dominican … I say Mass …

And he lists many members of his family, and asks for
a drink.

The same: Give me some wine!

And they give him wine, and he says:

The same: Oh, I hurt everywhere …

And he says nothing more the rest of the night, but suffered on, with the candles lit. And daybreak came, and they opened the windows and put out the candles. And he still kept silent. And they tell him not to play the fool, and he says:

The same: Oh, I'm dying … I'm dying …

And they asked him why he was arrested, and he says:

The same: I'm dead, I can't stand it anymore, O God!

And they tell him not to play the fool, and he says:

The same: I'm dying.

And the Lord Judges command that the torture be stayed, and that he be placed in a chair, and that was done, and as he was sitting down he says that he wants to piss, and they take him to the latrines near the torture chamber. And the third hour came, and they were about to put him back on the rack, and he says:

The same: Wait, brothers!

And once on the rack, he says nothing more, and he stayed there, suffering, calm, and silent. Then he asked that they lift his feet up a bit because they hurt badly, and they did it, and he rested quietly. And the Lord Judges asked him if he wished to sleep, and he says:

The same: Oh, yes!

And they tell him that if he will speak they will let him sleep as much as he wants, and he says nothing.

*

*   *

[Confrontation with another accused]

And then they let him get down to eat and drink and go to
the latrines, which took an hour, and they put him back
on the rack, and he says:
The same: What do you want of me?
And he appeared not to feel the pain any longer, and he
said nothing.
And the Lord Judges, hearing that he had asked for some
eggs to eat, had him given three on a plate, and when
they asked him if he wanted anything to drink, he said
yes, and they gave him some wine, and the Lord Judges
said that they would give him more if he would speak,
and they announced to him that they were going to start
the torture again, and he says:
The same: Leave me alone!
And they ask him why he is so preoccupied with his body,
and he answers:
The same: The soul is immortal.
And all the time he kept repeating:
The same: I'm dying, I'm dying …
And the Lord Judges ordered him to be taken down,
cleaned up, dressed, and taken back to his cell, and the
torture had lasted thirty-six hours.

[*Signed*] Johannes Camillus Pretiotus
Notary in Ecclesiastical Trials and Transactions of
the Archiepiscopal Tribunal of Naples

*

*   *

And a warden charged with taking the prisoner back and consigning him to the jailers of the Castel heard him say as they were crossing the royal hall:
The same: And they thought I'd be asshole enough to talk.

Official reports 345, 402, 404, 395
(Luigi Amabile, *Fra Tommaso Campanella*,
Naples, 1882)

MARGUERITE YOURCENAR (1903–1987) was a Belgian-born novelist, essayist, and short-story writer who became the first woman inducted into the Académie Française. Educated in French Flanders, she traveled extensively before permanently settling in the United States and establishing her home, Petite Plaisance, in Northeast Harbor, Maine, in 1950. Her literary works, known for their lyrical prose, depth of inquiry, and inventive speculation, often reimagine historical figures and eras, with *Memoirs of Hadrian* (1951) and *The Abyss* (1968) among her most acclaimed novels.

JOHN KNIGHT is a writer and editor whose work has appeared in *The New York Times Book Review*, *The Paris Review Daily*, *New York* magazine, *Nautilus*, and *Music & Literature*. He holds a PhD in comparative literature and serves as the executive director of Historic Harrisville, Inc., in New Hampshire, where he lives with his wife and children.

A Dream of Stone
Marguerite Yourcenar

Published by
David Zwirner Books
520 West 20th Street, 2nd Floor
New York, New York 10011
+ 1 212 727 2070
davidzwirnerbooks.com

Editor: Elizabeth Gordon
Proofreader: Anna Drozda

Design: Michael Dyer/Remake
Production manager: Luke Chase
Color separations: VeronaLibri,
Verona
Printing: VeronaLibri, Verona

Typeface: Arnhem
Paper: Holmen Book Cream, 80 gsm

Publication © 2025
David Zwirner Books

Distributed in the United States
and Canada by
Simon & Schuster, Inc.
1230 Avenue of the Americas
New York, New York 10020
simonandschuster.com

Distributed outside the
United States and Canada by
Thames & Hudson, Ltd.
6–24 Britannia Street
London WC1X 9JD
thamesandhudson.com

ISBN 978-1-64423-171-5

Library of Congress
Control Number: 2025936004

Printed in Italy

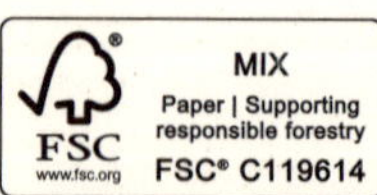